JOURNEY TO 3D ART & DESIGN

College Admissions & Profiles

Rachel A. Winston, Ph.D.

ISBN 978-1946432827 (hardback); 978-1946432810 (paperback); 978-1946432834 (e-book)

LCCN: 2022909744

Lizard Publishing, 7700 Irvine Center Drive, Suite 800, Irvine, CA 92618 *www.lizard-publishing.com*

Lizard Publishing creates, designs, produces, and distributes books and resources to provide academic, admissions, and career information. Our mental process is fueled by three tenets:

- Ignite the hunger to learn and the passion to make a difference
- Illuminate the expanse of knowledge by sharing cutting edge thinking
- Innovate to create a world that makes the transition from dreams to reality

We work with academic leaders who transform the educational landscape to publish relevant content and advise students of their educational and professional options, with the aim of developing 21st-century learners and leaders. We also work with students to publish their books and present widely diverse ideas to the college/graduate school-bound community. With headquarters in Irvine, California, Lizard Publishing works virtually with authors to edit, publish, and distribute both hard copy and paperback books.

This book was published in the U.S.A. Lizard Publishing is a premium quality provider of educational reference, career guidance, and motivational publications/merchandise for global learners, educators, and stakeholders in education.

Book design by Michelle Tahan *www.michelletahan.com*

Book formatting by Obinna Chinemerem Ozuo

Book website: *www.collegelizard.com*

LIZARD PUBLISHING

This book is dedicated to Joey Hanzich and Chase Heger, two students with extraordinary talents who never had the chance to fulfill their potential.

ACKNOWLEDGMENTS

There is never enough room to acknowledge every person. Numerous people contributed to my perspective about art. Students, faculty, counselors, and researchers assisted in enhancing my knowledge base or taught me indelible lessons. Over a lifetime of experiences working with students, I am wiser and more worldly.

I gratefully acknowledge Michelle Tahan, Jasmine Jhunjhnuwala, E. Liz Kim, and Jacqueline Xu, as well as my family, friends, colleagues, and professors. With profound gratitude, I also acknowledge those I have known in the art world.

As a faculty member in the UCLA College Counseling Certificate Program, I met many dedicated counselors who spend their lives serving and supporting students. Meaningful contributions to the book have been made indirectly by admissions representatives, college counselors, and faculty members who took a special interest in this book's success.

I would also like to thank the thousands of students I have taught, counseled, or supported in my nearly four decades of service.

"If I see so far, it is because I stand on the shoulders of giants."
Isaac Newton

Isaac Newton once said, "If I see so far, it is because I stand on the shoulders of giants." A few of those giants whose broad shoulders lifted me higher and helped teach invaluable lessons include Yulia Fomenko, Elizabeth Venturini, Daniel Wolf, Victoria Dozer, Desiree Moshayedi, Mariel Johnson, Tamar Nicherie, Cecilia Yang, Kendall May, Chenoa Robbins, Rachel Sobel, Samantha Wolf, Elaine Brewster, Stephanie Tahan, Gabriela Diller, and Regina DeBilio.

Finally, there would be no book on 3D art and design schools and no career in college admissions counseling without the support of Robert Helmer, whose tireless efforts support me every single day.

ABOUT THE AUTHOR

D r. Rachel A. Winston is a tireless student advocate. She has served the educational community as a university professor, college advisor, statistician, researcher, author, cryptanalyst, motivational speaker, publishing executive, and lifelong student. As one of the leading experts in college counseling and an award-winning faculty member, Dr. Winston has spent her lifetime learning, teaching, mentoring, and coaching students. Her counseling practice centers around college admissions, college essays, portfolios, and intellectual conversations about life and career pursuits.

She started college at thirteen and graduated from college programs in such widely ranging disciplines as chemistry, mathematics, computers, liberal arts, international relations, negotiation, conflict resolution, peacebuilding, business administration, higher education leadership, interpreting, college counseling, and publishing. Throughout her education, she attended and graduated from Harvard, University of Chicago, University of Texas, GWU, UCLA, Syracuse, CSUF, CSUDH, Pepperdine, Claremont Graduate University, and Gallaudet University.

Her position working in Washington, D.C. on Capitol Hill and with the White House in the 1980s took her to approximately a hundred universities training campaign managers at colleges from Colorado to California, thoroughly dotting the western states. Later, she led college tours with students and their families on road trips throughout the United States. She has taught or counseled thousands of students over her career and speaks at conferences and academic programs throughout the world.

As a professor and avid writer for numerous publications, she won the 2012 McFarland Literary Achievement Award, Bletchley Park Cryptanalyst Award, and numerous other awards, including Faculty Member of the Year, Leadership Tomorrow Leader of the Year, and college service and leadership awards. While studying Human Capital at Claremont Graduate University, she was a scholarship recipient at the Drucker School of Management. She was also elected to the statewide Board of Governors for the Faculty Association for California Community Colleges, where she served on the executive committee.

She also served as a faculty member for the UCLA College Counselor Certificate Program, the Director of Mathematics at Brandman University, and Embry Riddle Aeronautical University, Chapman University, Cal State Fullerton, and a handful of California Community Colleges, including Cerro Coso College where she represented the entire faculty as the Academic Senate President and retired in 2016. Over her career, she taught mathematics online, on television, live interactive satellite, telecourses, and in large and small lecture halls.

AUTHOR'S NOTE

You are reading this book because you are considering admission to colleges where you open the doors to the world of art, design, and creativity. Whatever route you took to get to this point, you are in the right place. Right now, you need to gather information to make informed decisions.

While many people offer advice, suggestions differ. Friends will tell you the 'right' way or the way their neighbor was accepted. Graciously accept this anecdotal information, pursuing imaginative artistry with your heart and mind as you commit to learning more.

Dig deeper to consider both expert and current information from counselors who have worked with hundreds of students. Changes in programs, curricula, requirements, and links happen each year.

Doublecheck each program's specifics yourself. Each school's profile information is current as of June 2022. However, since researching this book, changes may have taken place. There are other college guidebooks written by talented and experienced counselors, though none like this book on college programs for 3D art and design.

> "We are what we think. All that we are arises with our thoughts. With our thoughts, we make the world."
> — Buddha

This book, providing lists of colleges, admissions information, and profiles, is different in that it also offers unique tidbits. I hope you find the information valuable. Your job is to begin early by assembling lists of possible schools to consider. Create a road map and set yourself on a clear path.

If you see an error in this book or even a suggestion for a future edition, please write to Dr. Rachel A. Winston at collegeguide@yahoo.com. We will fix the entry with the next printed version. All of that said, this book was written with you in mind.

This book contains a wealth of information on the Internet with free downloads, FAQs, testimonials, and offers to help you with your applications. Some advisors are knowledgeable and provide valuable assistance. Unfortunately, students and parents hunt around the web, searching for a tremendous number of hours to seek the information they need. This book aims to resolve this problem with college admissions data and profiles to make your search easier.

For now, though, I will assume you want to attend college to study 3D art and design and are exploring this book to find a program that will get you on your way toward your goal. You are undoubtedly a talented candidate who is willing to work very hard. Creative mental exploration is virtually a prerequisite for all art programs.

As you investigate colleges, you might find that some programs are listed in different college departments. Either way, this book will help you reach your goal. Applying to and writing essays for each application will require research to determine which program is right for you and the specific reasons you are a good fit.

While you might believe that art-focused colleges are relatively similar, each program's nuances make them very different. These small differences may seem confusing. My goal with this book is to demystify the information and process.

CONTENTS

Chapter 1: Craft, Analyze, Form, and Engage — 1

Chapter 2: Exploring The Past and Present Of 3D Art & Design — 7

Chapter 3: Sculpture, Ceramics, Glass, & Jewelry: Academic Preparation & Career Options — 13

Chapter 4: School & Life Experiences: Internships & Programs For High School and College Students — 23

Chapter 5: University Options: College Programs For 3D Art & Design — 39

Chapter 6: What Is The Difference Between AN AA, AS, BA, BS, BFA, and MFA? — 55

Chapter 7: College Admissions: Terms, Data, Applications, Tests, and Essays — 65

Chapter 8: Financial Aid And Scholarships: Finding Money To Pay For College — 91

Chapter 9: Supplemental Materials And Portfolios For 3D Art & Design Programs — 99

Chapter 10: Post Pandemic Employment Outlook: Statistics and Economic Projections — 107

Chapter 11: Next Steps: Preparation and Real-World Skills — 115

Chapter 12: Region One - Northeast   128

Chapter 13: Region Two - Midwest   156

Chapter 14: Region Three - South   172

Chapter 15: Region Four - West   182

Chapter 16: 3D Art Schools by City/State   196

Chapter 17: 3D Art Schools by Average GPA and Average Test Score   200

Chapter 18: Top 15 Schools In Drawing and Painting   206

Chapter 19: Top Glassblowing Programs   208

Chapter 20: Top 20 Graduate Schools For Sculpture   210

Chapter 21: Top 40 Jewelry & Metal Arts Programs   212

Index   226

CHAPTER 1

CRAFT, ANALYZE, FORM, AND ENGAGE

"Patience is also a form of action."

– Auguste Rodin

I magine a job in which you create one-of-a-kind treasured objects out of materials that you cut, carve, shape, and mold. In a world of never-ending experimentation, the only limits are the bounds of your imagination. Quite literally, 3D works of art are often extraordinary, exceptional, and fantastical. Sculptures carved out of the face of a rock, hotels carved out of ice, or metal twisted into a 30-foot-tall bronze spider with marble eggs are a few amazing works of art. You are embarking on a journey to discover your passion, evoke deep-seated feelings, and share the meanings behind your work with others.

Three-dimensional art offers a uniquely powerful forum for self-expression. There is no place to hide since the 3D art can be seen from all sides. Individuals can look around a physical piece, viewing the object from multiple angles. From the artistic designs of glassblowers in Murano, Italy, knife makers in Tibet, China, and leather tanners in Fes, Morocco to the jade lapidaries of Hokitika, New Zealand, tanzanite artisans in Arusha, Tanzania, and rug makers of Istanbul, Turkey, 3D art forms abound with flair and excitement. Every home and every office should have some form of 3D art.

In college, try out various media. This is your chance to dabble in as many art forms as possible. You may be driven to choose glass, wood, clay, porcelain, marble, brass, precious metals, leather, stones, or some other form. Yet, college is a time for experimentation. Maybe you will discover a mixed media calling you have never before considered.

Take internships for a couple of months in Italy, Tibet, Morocco, New Zealand, Tanzania, or Turkey. Experiment with shapes and forms while you explore the avenues you find most appealing. Study abroad opportunities offer exciting first-hand looks at craftspeople in Africa, Asia, Europe, and South America. Venture out to the Alaska World Ice Art Championships in Fairbanks, be wowed at the Harbin Ice Festival in China, attend the Sapporo Snow Festival in Japan, or go to Banff, Canada to see the Ice Magic Festival. For another mesmerizing 3D immersion, stay

for a few nights in the Kirkenes Snow Hotel in Norway, Hotel of Ice in Romania, Snow Village in Finland, or the Ice Hotel in Japan or Sweden.

Endless fun and magical experiences exist in the 3D world. The Metaverse will likely offer you new vistas to explore where you can take your art even further. What if you turned your artistic creations into 4D sensations with emotion?

In whatever way you choose to use your talents, you will contemplate what you want to create and embark on your journey. This chapter is entitled "Craft, Analyze, Form, and Engage", meaning that you will dive into the deep end and swim among the colorful fish and breathtaking coral. Fanned by bright green seaweed and tantalized by swimming creatures in your new paradise, you will never have a dull moment.

Everything you try, whether or not the result is a masterpiece, will be an opportunity to play. Sure, there is real work involved but you will get guidance along the way. You will undoubtedly make mistakes. Also, this career pursuit will require skills in areas like branding, marketing, and advertising. However, if you hunger to create and you love to explore different media, head this way.

SCULPTURE

From *Christ the Redeemer*'s art deco style in Rio de Janeiro, Brazil, created by French sculptor Paul Landowski, to the soldiers, horses, and chariots at the Terracotta Warrior exhibit in Xian, China, sculpture lifts people's amazement in that breathtaking moment. Traversing Corcovado, the 2,239-foot mountain in Brazil through the Tijuca Forest up to the 125-foot statue of Jesus is a surreal experience. Walking along the massive grounds of Xi'an's Qin Tomb Terracotta Warriors and Horses and viewing the pits where molded, fired, assembled, and painted statues stand is awe-inspiring. If you endeavor to create lasting treasures of glass, metal, clay, wood, porcelain, or other material, 3D art and design is the right field for you.

INCREDIBLE 3D FIGURES

The most famous sculptures are immediately recognizable for their uniqueness. Powerful and provocative, these bold works from marble to metal are timeless. The physical presence of these unmissable sculptures, like the fifty listed below, astound visitors every day. While there are hundreds of additional amazing sculptures, there is no space to list them all. However, these are a few you should see in your lifetime.

50 STATUES TO SEE IN YOUR LIFETIME

Venus of Willendorf, Vienna, Austria

The Manneken Pis, Brussels, Belgium

Christ The Redeemer, Rio de Janeiro, Brazil

Moai, Rapa Nui, Easter Island, Chile

Spring Temple Buddha, Lushan, China

Leshan Giant Buddha, Sichuan, China

The Terracotta Army, Xi'an, China

Tian Ian Buddha, Lantau Island, China

Little Mermaid, Copenhagen, Denmark

Great Sphinx of Giza, near Cairo, Egypt

The Thinker, Paris, France

Venus de Milo, Paris, France

Les Voyageurs, Marseilles, France

Winged Victory of Samothrace, Paris, France

Nefertiti Bust, Berlin, Germany

Terrace of the Lions, Delos Island, Greece

Shoes on the Danube Bank, Budapest, Hungary

The Statue of Unity, Gujrat, India

Apollo & Daphne, Rome, Italy

The Capitoline Wolf, Rome, Italy

Christ of the Abyss, Genoa, Italy

The David, Florence, Italy

The Ecstasy of Saint Teresa, Rome, Italy

Perseus with the Head of Medusa, Florence, Italy

Rape of Prosperina, Rome, Italy

Olmec Colossal Heads, San Lorenzo, Mexico

The Monument of an Anonymous Passerby, Wroclaw, Poland

Force of Nature, Doha, Qatar

Monument to Mihai Eminescu, Iasi, Romania

The Motherland Calls, Volgograd, Russia

People of the River, Singapore

Nelson Mandela, Cape Town, South Africa

Maman, Bilbao, Spain

The Statues of Mount Nemrut, Adiyaman, Turkey

The Motherland Monument, Kyiv, Ukraine

The Independence Monument, Kyiv, Ukraine

The Angel of the North, Gateshead, England, UK

The Discus Thrower (Discobolus), London, England, UK

The Kelpies, Falkirk, Scotland, UK

Break Through From Your Mold, Philadelphia, PA, USA

Cloud Gate, Chicago, IL, USA

Expansion, New York, NY, USA

The Knotted Gun, New York, NY, USA

Lincoln Memorial, Washington, D.C., USA

Mount Rushmore, Keystone, SD, USA

Metalmorphosis, Charlotte, NC, USA

Statue Of Liberty, New York, NY, USA

Truth is Beauty, Burning Man, NV, USA

Augustus Prima Porta, Vatican City

The Pietà, Vatican City

CHAPTER 2

EXPLORING THE PAST AND PRESENT OF 3D ART & DESIGN

"You can't use up creativity. The more you use, the more you have."

– Maya Angelou

The enduring legacy of amazing art resonates, leaving people with an enduring *je ne sais quoi* memory. A lingering sense, feeling, or emotion emerges viewing artwork that defies imagination, stopping your breath for a moment and making you stare in awe. One example is *Shoes on the Danube Bank* in Budapest, Hungary. Sixty pairs of bronze shoes rest at the river's edge depicting the 3,500 people ordered to remove their shoes before they were shot, and their bodies fell into the Danube River.

Throughout history, sculptures were created to leave a lasting memory of an event, recognize a belief system, or honor the legacy of a hero. Other times, the work presented a transdisciplinary vision, exquisite craftsmanship, or uncanny intricacy.

Art is a uniquely human activity, presented in a wide range of forms, revealing clues about society at various points in history. From cave paintings and clay figurines, art has a long legacy and is often the only lasting depiction of civilizations long gone.

ORIGINS OF ART

The origins of art lie within Africa. Art served as a tool to communicate and preserve ideas and innovations. With an aesthetic appeal, creatively designed symbols and patterns defined humans' unique characteristics. Ideas and ways of life passed from generation to generation. Scientists believe that the Neanderthal made early petroglyphs, the first art known to exist approximately 65,000 years ago. Patterns with color, skin colorings with ochre, and beads for decoration were likely the early forms of art, though little information is available.

Homo sapiens migrated from Africa approximately 45,000 years ago as determined by artifacts found in Europe. Migrations continued to Asia too. New findings, though, show that the oldest cave painting, 45,500 years old, was found in Indonesia and etchings found in Germany are thought to be 51,000 years old.[1] Thousands of years later, 2D and 3D art emerged with curves, lines, products, tools, and manmade bowls. Examples of art appeared in other forms too, including European cave paintings and decorations. Written records were also found, providing documented evidence of early forms of music, dance, storytelling, and poetry.

With such a long history and trillions of examples produced over the millennia, humans' fascination for art offer insights into the evolution of creative inspirations. Today, art takes on a widening array of possibilities.

USING NEW TECHNOLOGIES TO AWE AND INSPIRE

This moment is exciting. New paradigms of art emerge as technology expands, disrupting every facet of life. Thus, we live in a time when our rapidly changing technologies require that we think differently and consider art from a new pair of glasses. The future of humanity and all other living things depends on those who can think past today, imagine tomorrow, and solve problems along the way. We live at a critical juncture where 5G, 6G, and 7G will mesh with digital currencies and Metaverse spaces. We will barely recognize our current existence by 2050. Much of that transformation will happen as a function of innovators who will invent tomorrow.

1   Amy McDermott, 2021. "What was the first 'art'? How would we know?" PNAS, October 27, 2021. https://www.pnas.org/doi/10.1073/pnas.2117561118

CHALLENGING CONVENTION

The definition of unique is to be different. So, challenge convention. Take a different path. Uninhibited creativity is fundamental to art, especially with 3D materials that add another dimension. Inquisitive experimentation is integral to your quest to become an artist as you blaze a trail toward your distinctive style. However, not everything you try will work. Some ideas will suffer the slings and arrows of those around you who question your abilities or simply cannot understand your creations. You can continue unabated or try something new. Feedback is good, though it sometimes stings. Use the feedback or not.

This is your journey, not theirs. After all, this is art. It is your imagination you are letting loose. And, in this space of vulnerability, you may feel insecure. Keep pushing through to new possibilities. Remember that, while Vincent van Gogh may be one of the greatest painters of all time, the Dutch post-impressionist suffered enormous hardships in his personal and professional life. Sadly, he achieved worldwide fame and success after his lifetime.

Success is sometimes the outcome of a whole string of failures.

– Vincent van Gogh

Embodying deep and complex thinking, artists often struggle with the world around them. People in society never truly understand their persistent efforts to push boundaries, unquenchable hunger to experiment, and ceaseless need for excellence. Unable to find perfection in themselves, they pour their mental energies into their art. Other times, their high standards lead them to unwittingly push away the people they care for the most.

Creative and intellectual, artists often pursue 3D works to investigate and resolve challenges of shape and form. Throughout your college experience, you will develop advanced 3D skills with a highly sophisticated sense of fundamental elements and principles in art and design. You will investigate material, molding, and composition challenges while adding shape, texture, and color. You will learn how to mix media with soft and hard elements, contrasting each form using elements of texture, transparency, and intricate details.

Synthesizing your ideas through the visual interrelationships, you will translate the themes of your work into expressions of your artistic passion. Each composition will be distinct but will fit into a body of your work as you explore new media and examine the challenges and opportunities of each. You will also learn how to formulate your ideas into a cohesive and concise description of your thought process. All along the way, you will learn as much about yourself as you do about the artistic media.

HOPE AND PRAGMATISM

As an experimentalist, you will construct the foundation for civilization's future. Begin this journey by stepping into the possibilities of today and the augmented realities of tomorrow. There are many directions you can take with your creative artistry. The combination of complex concepts will add to the challenge and intrigue of your career. The programs and colleges profiled in this book offer varied paths for you to explore. Choose the direction that makes the most sense to you. The information contained within will lead you on your way.

Every block of stone has a statue inside it
and it is the task of the sculptor to discover it.

- Michelangelo

CHAPTER 3

SCULPTURE, CERAMICS, GLASS, & JEWELRY: ACADEMIC PREPARATION & CAREER OPTIONS

"All our dreams can come true if we have the courage to pursue them."

– Walt Disney

You are headed toward art mastery. To gain admission to your dream college you must be smart and talented. Even if the admission's requirements do not require a portfolio, and many do, to be successful, there are numerous preparatory skills you must develop as if you were presenting your work to a committee. Plan for your future now. Talent is only the beginning.

In high school, or college if you plan to transfer into a program, you must build solid skills in studio training inside and/or outside of school. The more exceptional artwork you can present to an admissions committee within their guidelines the better. Some mix of drawing, painting, ceramics, sculpture, 3-D design, and digital art are key components of a portfolio, though not all of these skills are necessary. Some applicants have never taken a course in jewelry design or sculpture and are not penalized. Nevertheless, foundational skills in art theory and practice are important.

COMPELLING REASONS TO STUDY 3D ART & DESIGN

1. Freedom of creative expression
2. Mind explosion of ideas and possibilities
3. Love for experimentation with colors, forms, styles, shapes, and media
4. Sensory experience when witnessing captivating imagery
5. Emotional feeling that beckons you into art's space
6. The chance to turn your love into a lifetime career
7. Self-expression, self-confidence, and self-awareness
8. Individuality, unique flair, and distinctive style

IS ATTENDING COLLEGE TO STUDY
CLAY, GLASS, METAL, & MIXED MATERIALS WORTH IT?

Art has the power to relieve stress and awaken the senses. School is often unempowering for those who are disenchanted with memorizing chapters of text, reading endless books, and solving problems that seem to have no practical use. Learning math, science, and history present a one-size-fits-all model, where everyone marches in line and dutifully follows the requirements. However, there is something useful, presentable, and magical about art.

In its many forms, art enlivens. If you have practiced art, you may have a favorite medium to express yourself and define your distinct style. However, with a degree concentrated on art and design, you will learn many additional styles and techniques.

The immersive college experience will expose you to the practices of great artists and alternative methodologies of contemporary idea generators today. You will discover a wide range of options in each art class while determining the styles and techniques you prefer. Instructors, guest lecturers, and workshop hosts will help you continue to improve your skills while offering you feedback to go to the next level.

CAN ARTISTS MAKE A LIVING?

Since money and time are valuable commodities, the question of worth, value, and future income always crop up in my college counseling sessions. Consider your future wisely before making such a big decision, though I believe that "where there is a will, there is a way." This means, of course, that you must be dedicated to your craft, have a vision for where you are headed, be persistent in taking opportunities to practice, and have the wisdom to make smart choices.

In a world where social media can connect you to customers, you can display your art through many different sites without leaving your studio, which may be your home or apartment. You may choose to be an intrepid frontrunner by creating a gallery in the Metaverse and selling your artwork using NFTs, bitcoin, or another digital payment system.

Amazing college professors who are successful in their own right will suggest ways to sell your art and may even link you to their contacts. In the process, you will discover your brand of professionalism along with a calling card of images that allow others to understand what you offer.

"THERE IS NO ROYAL ROAD TO GEOMETRY" - EUCLID

When a student asked Euclid if there was an easier way to learn geometry, he cautioned that discipline and persistence are essential. Hard work is absolutely necessary. Additionally, there is no one way to succeed, just as there is no one way to design. You may choose to draw images for a company, sell your creations, teach others fine arts, or support other artists by sharing your wisdom. Either way, art is a versatile skill. Other professional options include arts management, museum studies, television, entertainment, fashion, education, art therapy, and much more.

You could manage an art store, create an online webstore, critique art, or help others market their art. Museums also have positions that require the knowledge of trained artists.

Teaching is often considered a fallback. Yet, many people who choose to teach are inspired by the innocence and dreams of young artists. Finally, art therapy has excellent potential to make a difference in someone's life. So many people were demoralized by the pandemic and could not find their way forward toward hope and possibility. You could support others to find their peace of mind. My point is that, as you develop your skills, your talent is not wasted, not lost, not valueless. You can be a source of empowerment and strength for others.

ARTS MANAGEMENT

This field has grown in the past decade as more people seek ways to contemplate life through art. The job of an arts manager is to know and understand art while also having a business sense to manage a private or public art institution. Thus, arts managers efficiently run the business and share the creative inspirations of artists, performers, or designers. With skills in planning events, managing talent, envisioning space, communicating messages, and hosting guests, you will serve society in significant ways. For example, suppose you want to inspire both artists and patrons alike, giving artists the freedom to express themselves while offering visitors or purchasers the chance to learn, identify, feel, and imagine. In that case, arts management is an excellent profession, and it can pay well.

ARTS/ENTERTAINMENT AGENT

This profession is perfect for the person who is inspired to help artists find locations to promote, show, and sell their artwork. Many times, artists consume themselves in their art. They become immersed in the vision and technical precision of their craft. However, they are not skilled in public relations, advertising, promotion, website development, social media, and the legal aspects of contracts, releases, and intellectual property. Many artists want to focus on their art rather than pounding the pavement to find shows, exhibitions, events, venues, and other opportunities. Here, an agent may be invaluable.

An arts/entertainment agent ensures that excellent art of all kinds has a platform to be seen. Imagine for a moment how many thousands of extraordinarily talented artists exist whose work is never seen except possibly among a small enclave of other talented artists or friends. Thus, those who are 'successful' are 'discovered' or promoted. They are not always the best artists. You might find representing talented people uplifting. Otherwise, you might contract with an arts/entertainment agent yourself.

FASHION DESIGN, TEXTILE DESIGN, AND MERCHANDISING

Artists with an eye for color, style, and design often express this through their own hair, clothing, or accessories. Often, they enjoy pondering other individuals' attires as models of fashion or ways to augment their look. Starting with envisioning and sketching fabric designs before they are woven, or designing them after the cloth is created, there is an immense amount of artistry involved with clothing creation. Attending fashion shows, buying next season's designs, marketing outfits, and displaying items in stores takes the flair of a creative mind. Individuals with these interests may discover that segments of the fashion industry are immensely appealing.

TEACHING, EDUCATION, AND TRAINING

Kids clamor to create. Their imaginations run wild with ideas. Self-expression and exploration through art offer people young and old the chance to put their ideas onto paper, a computer, or a still or moving medium like photography or film. Some perform in voice, dance, and acting. As a result, there are numerous jobs in private and public education. Schools everywhere hire art teachers. Families hire art coaches. Private studios conduct workshops and training. College art professors can make $100,000/year teaching students while continuing to practice their craft.

In the United States, there were approximately 130,000 public and private K-12 schools in 2021, according to the National Center for Educational Statistics. Furthermore, during the 2019-2020 school year, there were 3,982 degree-granting higher education colleges and universities - 2,679 4-year and 1,303 2-year institutions.[1] In California alone, during the 2020-2021 school year, there were 10,545 K-12 public schools and another 1,296 charter schools.[2] Thus, there are numerous schools in which you may choose to work.

---

1   NCES, "Digest of Education Statistics," U.S. Department of Education, 2020 Tables and Figures, https://nces. ed.gov/programs/digest/d20/tables/dt20_317.10.asp

2   California Department of Education, "Fingertip Facts on Education in California", 2020-2021, https://www.cde. ca.gov/ds/ad/ceffingertipfacts.asp

ART THERAPY

Art therapists are clinicians who support people of all ages as mental health practitioners. They provide services and counseling through the active practice of art-making and other creative processes. Art can be a healing power, allowing individuals to improve their physical and mental abilities while reducing both stress and conflict and improving both self-esteem and self-awareness. Using applied psychology, art therapists improve the human experience in a psychotherapeutic relationship. Art therapists must be credentialed and certified to practice in hospitals, schools, veteran's clinics, private practice, rehabilitation centers, psychiatric facilities, community clinics, crisis centers, forensic institutions, and senior communities.

To become an art therapist, you must attend graduate school and earn a master's or doctoral degree. However, there are undergraduate programs in art therapy that can get you on your way. A Master of Arts in Art Therapy can also lead to a Master of Arts in Marriage and Family Studies or a Ph.D. in Art Therapy. Most graduate programs prepare graduates to sit for the Art Therapy Registration (ATR), Licensed Creative Arts Therapist (LCAT), and Licensed Professional Clinical Counselor (LPCC).

UNDERGRADUATE ART THERAPY PROGRAMS
AMERICAN ART THERAPY ASSOCIATION

Anna Maria College (MA)

Capital University (OH)

Converse College (SC)

Edgewood College (WI)

Long Island University, Post Campus (NY)

Mars Hill University (NC)

Mercyhurst University (PA)

Millikin University (IL)

Mount Mary University (WI)

Notre Dame of Maryland Univ. (MD)

Russell Sage College (NY)

Seton Hill University (PA)

St. Thomas Aquinas College (NY)

Temple University (PA)

University of the Arts (PA)

University of Tampa (FL)

Ursuline College (OH)

CAAHEP ACCREDITED GRADUATE ART THERAPY PROGRAMS[3]

Adler Graduate School (MN)

Albertus Magnus College (CT)

Antioch University Seattle (WA)

Caldwell University (NJ)

Drexel University (PA)

Eastern Virginia Medical School (VA)

Edinboro University (PA)

Emporia State University (KS)

Florida State University (FL)

George Washington University (DC)

Hofstra University (NY)

Indiana Univ.-Purdue Univ.-IUPUI (IN)

Lewis & Clark College (OR)

Long Island University – Post (NY)

Loyola Marymount University (CA)

Maywood University (PA)

Naropa University (CO)

Nazareth College (NY)

New York University (NY)

Southern Illinois University (IL)

Southwestern College (NM)

Springfield College (MA)

St. Mary-of-the-Woods College (IN)

University of Louisville (KY)

Ursuline College (OH)

LIMITLESS POSSIBILITIES

The preparation you receive as an art student will not restrict you. One of my students went from painting to game design, which required a year of focused digital skills, but he now has an amazing job that he enjoys. Art and design skills are fundamental to any creative area. Your options will be completely open, providing you with the freedom to choose which direction you want to go.

The scope of art is expanding with new frontiers that offer opportunities never before imaginable. For example, new industries and manufacturing facilities need artists to imagine and invent advertising, products, tools, toys, fashions, graphics, and imagery on websites and soon the Metaverse. The ever-expanding need is why some colleges like Savannah College of Art and Design, Maryland Institute College of Art, and Ringling College of Art and Design have a dozen or more specialized majors in art, giving students the flexibility to adapt their program with new areas of interest.

Studying art will also keep you creative, allowing you to explore your evolving artistic style. Art is increasingly recognized as a valuable skill. If you are passionate about this pursuit, one day, your efforts will bear fruit!

CHAPTER 4

SCHOOL & LIFE EXPERIENCES: INTERNSHIPS & PROGRAMS FOR HIGH SCHOOL AND COLLEGE STUDENTS

"Happiness is like a butterfly; the more you chase it, the more it will elude you, but if you turn your attention to other things, it will come and sit softly on your shoulder."

– Henry David Thoreau

S tart early to gain drawing, ceramics, sculpture, and design experiences. Internships and summer programs are as important along your educational pathway as coursework. The lessons you learn from working collaboratively and collegially with other art and design-focused mentors may be different but equally important. Historian and scholar, W.E.B. DuBois (1868-1963), a founding member of the NAACP and the first Black American to earn a Ph.D. at Harvard said, "Education must not simply teach work - it must teach life." Your college, experiential, and life education go hand-in-hand, driven by purpose and foresight since life truly is a journey, not a destination.

WHY PARTICIPATE IN SUMMER PROGRAMS/INTERNSHIPS?

You should participate in summer programs and internships. While some students and parents chose these options to look good and show dedication, the real reason why you should participate is to develop your skills while obtaining constructive critique and feedback from specialists in the field. Discussions, seminars, studio work, and portfolio development are immensely valuable for your future pursuits. However, merely living on a campus and getting a feel for what college would be like cannot be understated.

Note: This list is not exhaustive, and it is not an endorsement of any program. Dates, program descriptions, and program length may be changed from year to year.

SUMMER CAMPS & PROGRAMS FOR ART, DESIGN, FILM, PHOTOGRAPHY, AND ARCHITECTURE

Alabama

Auburn University – Architecture Camp – Creative Writing – Industrial Design

One week – Three Session Options – Full Scholarships Available (apply by April 1)

Students produce designs working directly with professors.

Camp counselors support students with 24/7 questions, safety, and supervision.

Tuskegee University Taylor School of Architecture & Construction Science

Virtual Preview of Architecture and Construction at Tuskegee (V-PACT) 3-hour Virtual Program

Preview Architecture & Construction Science 2-Week Program

Arizona

Arcosanti – Re-Imagined Urbanism – 6-week discussion-based classes - AZ

Combining architecture and ecology (arcology), you can learn in the World's First Prototype Arcology.

Core values: (1) Frugality and Resourcefulness, (2) Ecological Accountability, (3) Experiential Learning, and (4) Leaving a Limited Footprint, Arcosanti is juxtaposed to mass consumerism, urban sprawl, unchecked consumption, and social isolation.

Arkansas

University of Arkansas – In Person & Virtual Design Camp – Fayetteville, AK

In-Person Grades 9-12 - design projects, studio groups, tours, & meetings with local designers.

No fee; completely remote; design camp lessons embedded; students are paired with a faculty member in a studio group.

Advanced Design Camp: students entering Grades 11-12, 2 weeks in Fayetteville

California

Academy of Art Institute – San Francisco

4-6 weeks – Advertising, Animation/VFX, Architecture, Fashion, Fine Art, Game Development, Graphic Design

Illustration, Industrial Design, Motion Pictures, Music Production, Photography, Writing for Film, TV, & Digital Media

California State Summer School of the Arts (CSSSA) – Sacramento, CA

Rigorous 4-week, pre-professional visual and performing arts 2D and 3D training program in painting, printmaking, sculpture, ceramics, digital media, and photography; scholarship possibility for CA residents. Grades 9 – 12.

Getty Museum – Paid Student Gallery Guide – Los Angeles, CA

Paid summer internship for teens ($2,400 in 2022). Learn the fundamentals of museums and public speaking while leading visitors around the grounds.

Also available – Open Call for teen photographers to share images, 8-week paid STEAM internship, and Summer Latin Academy at the Getty Villa to learn Latin

Laguna College of Art & Design Pre-College Program – Laguna Beach, CA

Animation, Sculpture, Drawing Fundamentals, Figure Drawing, Graphic Design

Otis College of Art and Design Summer of Art – Los Angeles, CA

Intensive 4-week program for students 15+ for portfolio and studio training in architecture, conceptual art, digital media, graphic design, and printmaking, with lectures and critiques. Merit and need-based scholarships are available.

School of Creative & Performing Arts (SOCAPA) – Occidental College (13-18-year-olds)

2-week, 3-week - learn Filmmaking, Screenwriting, Dance, Music, Photography

SCI-Arc (Southern California Institute of Architecture) Immersive 4-week Summer Program (Design Immersion Days) – Los Angeles

Introduction to the academic and professional world of architecture – Grades 9-12

Stanford University – 8-Week Summer Courses and 3-Week Arts Institute

Architecture, Art, Drawing, Dance, Creative Writing, Music, and Photography

UCLA Summer Jumpstart Summer Art Inst, Digital Media Arts Inst., Digital Filmmaking Inst., Game Lab Inst.

2-week program - Portfolio development– credit available

Drawing, Painting, Photography, Sculpture, Video Art, Animation, and Game Design

USC Summer Film, Writing, and Architecture Programs – Los Angeles

2-4-week program, "Creative Writing Workshop", "Comedy Performance", "Exploration into Architecture"

Connecticut

Summer Studio: Discovering Graphic Design (AIGA) – Bridgeport, CT

Free 4-week hands-on program for Bridgeport rising juniors and seniors

Week 1 – Music Festival Poster, Week 2 – Digital Media Poster

Week 3 – Animating Your Ideas, Week 4 – Portfolio Art for College Applications

District of Columbia

Catholic University School of Architecture and Planning

Summer High School Program - 2-week Residential (Two Session Options)

George Washington University Digital Storytelling Pre-College Program – July

Produce stories with smartphones, learn storyboarding, and broadcast through social media

Craft ideas, capture images, & create compelling content, including character development

Georgetown University – 1-week – Creative Writing – Publishing

Fiction, Short Story, Poetry, and Professional Writing; visit literary hubs

Florida

Florida Atlantic University – Boca Raton, FL and Ft. Lauderdale, FL

School of Architecture – July (Three Session Options)

July 3-week program for rising sophomores, juniors, seniors, and students in their first 2 years of college

Certificate of Completion Awarded – Enrollment on a first-come, first-served basis

Portfolio development, fabrication, architectural education, portfolio display, critique

Ringling College of Art and Design – Sarasota, FL

Intensive 4-week program focused on art and design including computer animation, creative writing, digital sculpting, entertainment design, fabrication, film directing/production, game art, game design, illustration, painting, photography, storyboarding, and virtual reality development.

University of Florida Design Exploration Program (DEP)

3-week Residential Immersion into the architectural studio environment.

Construction of studio design projects, teamwork, seminars, field trips, architectural theory.

University of Miami Summer Scholars, Explorations in Architecture & Design– Coral Gables, FL

3-week Residential program; 6 college credits; Design, Graphics, and Theory.

Architecture, Landscape Architecture, Historic Preservation; Urban Planning.

Studio experience with drawing, model making, drafting, CAD, visual analysis.

Georgia

Emory University – Atlanta, GA – 2-, 4-, 6-Week Writing Programs

Journalism, Dramatic Writing, Media & Politics, Psychology & Fiction

Georgia Institute of Technology Pre-College Design Program – Atlanta, GA

2-week Residential program – College of Design – Grades 11 & 12 (Two Session Options)

Architecture, Building Construction, Industrial Design, and Music Technology

Savannah College of Art & Design – Savannah, GA - SCAD 5-week Rising Star & SCAD courses

2-week College of Design Residential program –– Grades 11 & 12 - Courses include Advertising, Animation, Virtual Reality, Illustration, Storyboarding,

Photography, Painting, Fashion, Digital Film, Graphic Design, and Industrial Design

Illinois

Illinois Institute of Technology Summer Introduction to Architecture

2-week Experiment in Architecture for HS students – Comprehensive overview

1-week Exploration in Architecture for middle school students – studio-based, firm visits, field trips, projects.

Northwestern University – National HS Institute

5-week Film & Video, Music, Speech & Debate, Theatre

School of the Art Institute of Chicago – Early College Program for HS Students

1-, 2-, 4-week Residential programs in Painting, Drawing, Animation, Comics/ Graphic Novels, and Fashion Design.

Portfolio development programs; earn college credit. Full-tuition scholarships are available.

Southern Illinois University Carbondale – Kid Architecture

1-week Elementary Grades, Middle School & High School Architecture Camp

University of Illinois at Chicago Architecture - HiArch Summer High School Program

1-, 2-week (July) - HS students are introduced to the culture of architecture, design, thinking, and making.

University of Chicago Creative Writing Immersion

"Collegiate Writing: Awakening Into Consciousness" and "Creative Writing: Fiction"

Indiana

University of Notre Dame Summer Scholars Program

2-weeks HS Students – Film, Photography, Performing Arts - studios, seminars, and field trips

Iowa

Iowa State University – College of Design - HS Design Camps

1-week HS Students – Architecture, Studio/Fine Arts, Graphic Design, Interior Design, & Industrial Design

Maryland

Maryland Institute College of Art (MICA) – Baltimore, MD

2-, 3-, 5-week HS Students – Live instruction, studio time, workshops, artist talks, collaboration, feedback, critique, evaluation

Massachusetts

Boston College - Boston, MA – Creative Writing Seminar Program

3-week (July) Residential Program – HS Students – nonfiction, fiction, poetry – hone techniques

Create & edit the class literary journal and present writings at a public reading

Harvard University GSD Design Discovery– Cambridge, MA (Ages 18-mid-career professionals)

3-week Residential Program – Architecture, Landscape, Urban Planning & Design

Physical modeling, fabrication, assembly

Harvard Summer Program for High School Students

2-week non-credit program; 7-week college credit program (live in campus dorms)

Credit classes include: Creating Comics & Graphic Novels; Drawing & the Digital Age; Advertising, Landscape, & Visual Imagery; Creative Writing

Massachusetts College of Art & Design – 4-Week Art Immersion Program

Students take 3 foundation courses; closing exhibition

Massachusetts Institute of Technology – Urbaneframe – Cambridge, MA

HS Students - Summer Design-Build Project

CAD, drafting, sketching, mapping and context study, historical research, carpentry & construction

Tufts University – 6-Week Writing Intensive

Writing exercises, evaluation from professors, revise, develop papers that build on a theme

University of Massachusetts Amherst Pre-College – Amherst, MA

1-, 2-, 3-week Residential Intensives Grades 10-12

3-D Design, 3-D Animation, Building & Construction Technology; Combatting the Climate Crisis

Summer Engineering Institute, Summer Design Academy, Programming for Aspiring Scientists

Wellesley College – Wellesley, MA

2-week Residential Program - EXPLO Pre-College + Career for Grades 10-12

Three session options; Topics include – AI, Entrepreneurship, Engineering, Medicine, Law, CSI

Youth Design Boston (AIGA) – Boston, MA

Summer Graphic Design Internship & Mentoring Program

Michigan

Andrews University School of Architecture & Interior Design - Renaissance Kids – Berrien Springs, MI

Virtual Studio Projects; lecture; community build projects

Interlochen Center for the Arts – Summer Arts Camp – 1-6 Weeks

Creative Writing, Dance, Art, Motion Picture, Music, Theatre, Visual Arts

University of Michigan – Stamps School of Art & Design – BFA Preview

3-week (June/July)– HS Students – Creative retreat with state-of-the-art facilities & museum excursions

Missouri

Washington University in St. Louis – Creative Writing Institute and HS Summer Scholars Program

2-week program – fiction, nonfiction, and poetry; morning writer's workshops – editing and sharing work

5-8 week – Dance, Journalism, Photography, Music, Drama, Photojournalism

University of Missouri Kansas City – Department of Architecture, Urban Planning & Design MA

Design Discovery Program – Architecture, Interior Design, Landscape Architecture

3-day (July) Non-Residential Program – HS Students/Current College Students

Nebraska

University of Nebraska College of Architecture – Lincoln, NE

6-day (June) Residential Program – Grades 11 & 12 – Studio training; architectural design; scholarships

New Jersey

New Jersey Institute of Technology – Hillier College of Architecture & Design

1-week (July) Residential Program – HS Students – Architecture, Interior Design, Industrial Design, Digital Design

Summer Architecture + Design Programs (2 Start Dates)

New York

AIA New York – Center for Architecture

1-week (July) Residential Program – HS Students – Architecture

Programs for Grades 3-12 include Architectural Design Studio, Drawing Architecture, Rooftop Dwelling, Dream House, Treehouses, Skyscrapers, Green Island Home, Subway Architecture, Waterfront City, Parks & Playground Design, and Neighborhood Design

Columbia University - New York, NY – Summer Immersion

3-week July-August Residential Program – Architecture, Creative Writing, Drawing, Filmmaking, Photography, Theater, or Visual Arts

Cooper Union - New York, NY – Summer Art Intensive

4-week July-August Residential Programs – Portfolio Development, Exhibition, Anthology Publication

Animation, Creative Writing, Photography, Drawing, Graphic Design, & Stop Animation

Cornell University – Ithaca, NY – Precollege Studies and 3-Week Transmedia: Image, Sound, Motion Program

3-, 6-, 9-week June-August Residential Program; Drawing and New Media (collage, drawing, digital photography, screen printing, & video)

Architecture: Design Studio, Culture, and Society, Architectural Science & Technology

New York University Summer Art Intensive

4-week Immersive program in Digital & Video, Sculpture, or Visual Arts

Parsons School of Design – New York and Paris

4-week - Online and on-campus summer programs for students from 3rd grade to 12th

NYC - Portfolio building in 3-credit immersive Design, Studio Art, Photography, Illustration, Game Design

Paris Program – Design & Mgmt, Explorations in Drawing & Painting, Fashion Design

Rensselaer Polytechnic University – Troy, NY

Architecture Career Discovery Program

School of Creative & Performing Arts (SOCAPA) – New York (13-18-year-olds)

2-, 3-week - Learn Filmmaking, Screenwriting, Dance, Music, Photography

Syracuse University – Syracuse, NY – On-Campus and Online Programs for HS Students

2-, 3-, 6-week programs 3-D Studio Art; Sculpture; Architecture; Design Studies; Writing Immersion

Oklahoma

University of Oklahoma Architecture Summer Academy

1-week (June) Residential Program – HS Students – Architecture, Interior Design, Construction Science

Design in Action: Creativity, Innovation, and Sustainability Shaping the Built Environment

Pennsylvania

Carnegie Mellon University Pre-College Art Program - Pittsburgh, PA

3-, 4-, 6-week (July-August) Residential Program – Intensive Studio Studies

Portfolio development in Drawing, Sculpture, Animation, and Concept Studio Art

Chestnut Hill College Global Solutions Lab

Interactive Global Simulation, Electrifying Africa, & UN Sustainable Development Goals

1-week programs – HS Students – Intensive collaborative team solutions to big problems

Drexel University Westphal College of Media Arts & Design – Discovering Architecture

2-week Residential Program – HS Students – Intensive Studio Architecture Program

Visit prominent architectural, multi-disciplinary design offices; meet architects

Maywood University Pre-College Summer Workshop School of Architecture

2-week (July) Residential Program – HS Students – Design Your Future Architecture Program

Pennsylvania State University Architecture & Landscape Architecture Summer Camp

1-week (July) – HS Students –Architecture, Graphics, Design, and the Built Environment Program

Temple University Tyler School of Art and Architecture Pre-College Architecture Program

Architecture Institute – Philadelphia, PA

2-week (July-August) Residential Program – HS Students – Studio Architecture

Rhode Island

Brown University – 1-4 Weeks – Art Themed Courses

Creative Writing, Music, Studio Art, Art History

Rhode Island School of Design Pre-College School of Design – Providence, RI

6-week (June-July) Residential Program – HS Students – Foundational Art & Design Studies

Figure drawing, projects, trips, exhibitions

Roger Williams University High School Summer Academy in Architecture

4-week (July-August) Residential Program – Grades 11 & 12 – Explore Studio Architecture

Seminars, fieldwork, studio, portfolio development

South Carolina

Clemson University Pre-College School of Architecture Program

1-week (July-August) Residential Program – Grades 7-12

Engineering Design, Mechanical Engineering, Civil Engineering, Intelligent Vehicles, Materials Engineering

Tennessee

The University of Memphis Discovering Architecture + Design

1-day – HS Students – Design programs on architecture, interior design, and the built environment

The University of Tennessee, Knoxville College of Architecture + Design

1-week UT Summer Design Camp (July) Residential – HS Students

Immersive architecture, graphic design, and professional practice program

Vanderbilt Summer Academy – Nashville, TN – 3-Week Program

"Digital Storytelling", "Writing Fantasy Fiction", "Math & Music", "Writing Short Stories"

Texas

Texas Tech Anson L Clark Scholars Program – Research Area: Advertising, Architecture, Art, Dance, or Theatre

7-week – Grades 11 & 12 – Residential Program (must be 17 years old by start date) – no program fee

Intensive research-based program; $500 meal card; $750 tax-free stipend

University of Houston & Wonderworks Pre-College Summer Discovery Program

Hines College of Architecture & Design – Introduction to Architecture

6-week – HS Students – Design programs with hands-on studio, field trips, and portfolio workshop

The University of Texas at Austin Summer Design Camps – 2-D Game Design, 3-D Game Design, 3-D Animation/Motion

School of Design and Creative Technologies

1-week – HS Students – portfolio development and design

Vermont

School of Creative & Performing Arts (SOCAPA) – Burlington, VT (13-18-year-olds)

2-week, 3-week - learn Filmmaking, Screenwriting, Dance, Music, Photography

Virginia

Virginia Tech Inside Architecture + Design

1-week – HS Students – Hands-on design studio architecture program

Washington

DigiPen Academy – K-12 Animation, Film, Music, Game Design Summer Programs – Redmond, WA

1-week and 2-week programs, including Teen Art & Animation; Film Scoring Music & Sound Design; Video Game Development; Animation Masterclass

Wisconsin

The University of Wisconsin Milwaukee School of Architecture & Urban Planning

1-week – HS Students – Design program on architecture, interior design, and the built environment

During high school and college, you have the opportunity to explore your interests through summer programs, skill-building camps, and internships. Try out different fields you might not have considered before. You never really have the same chance to consider alternatives in quite the same way. Learn something new. There are hundreds of career areas you may never have considered. Have some fun while you are at it!

CHAPTER 5

UNIVERSITY OPTIONS: COLLEGE PROGRAMS FOR 3D ART & DESIGN

"It's not what you look at that matters, it's what you see."

– Henry David Thoreau

In the United States, more than 300 colleges offer a 4-year accredited degree in fine arts. Altogether, more than two million people in the United States have degrees in visual and performing arts, with about half specifically in visual arts. However, only about ten percent make the bulk of their income through art.

U.S. College Students – approximately 19.6 million

14.5 million attending public colleges;

5.14 million attending private colleges

2,679 4-year colleges; 1,303 2-year colleges

Another interesting statistic is that undergraduate enrollment dropped more than 4% from fall 2019 to fall 2020 and another 3.5% from fall 2020 to fall 2021, representing approximately a 1,500,000 loss of students during the pandemic. However, with test-optional admissions opening the door to more students without test scores or who test poorly, more students applied to the top schools.

TOP PROGRAMS IN METAL AND GLASS

1. Yale University
2. Rhode Island School of Design
3. School of the Art Inst. of Chicago
4. Columbia University
5. Bard College
6. Boston University
7. Maryland Institute College of Art
8. University of California, Los Angeles
9. California Institute of the Arts
10. Hunter College - CUNY
11. Pratt Institute
12. School of Visual Arts
13. Virginia Commonwealth University
14. Cranbrook Academy of Art
15. Temple University
16. Rutgers University

Everyone has heard about the top colleges fine arts. Yet, there are many more excellent programs. The colleges that offer *the most bachelor's degrees in Fine Art* each year are:

1. School of the Art Inst. of Chicago
2. Cal State Fullerton
3. Cal State Long Beach
4. University of North Texas
5. City University of New York
6. Florida State University
7. University of Central Florida
8. San Jose State University
9. Indiana University - IUPUI
10. Hunter College - CUNY

U.S. – ACCREDITED ART-CENTERED COLLEGES

United States

Art Academy of Cincinnati (OH)
ArtCenter College of Design (CA)
Art Institute of Boston (MA)
Art Institute of Pittsburgh (PA)
California College of the Arts (CA)
California Institute of the Arts (CA)
Cleveland Institute of Art (OH)
College for Creative Studies (MI)
Columbia College Chicago (IL)
Cooper Union (NY)
Corcoran Col. of Art & Design - GWU (DC)
Cornish College of the Arts (WA)
Fashion Institute of Technology (NY)
Kansas City Art Institute (MO)
Kendall College of Art & Design (MI)
Laguna College of Art & Design (CA)
Lyme Academy College of Fine Arts (CT)
Maine College of Art (ME)
Maryland Institute College of Art (MD)
Mass. College of Art & Design (MA)
Memphis College of Art (TN)

Milwaukee Institute of Art & Design (WI)
Minneapolis College of Art & Design (MN)
Montserrat College of Art (MA)
Moore College of Art & Design (PA)
New Hampshire Institute of Art (NH)
N. Michigan Univ. School of Art & Design (MI)
Oregon College of Art & Craft (OR)
Otis College of Art & Design (CA)
Pacific Northwest College of Art (OR)
Parsons School of Design (NY)
Pratt Institute (NY)
Rhode Island School of Design (RI)
Ringling College of Art & Design (FL)
San Francisco Art Institute (CA)
Savannah College of Art & Design (GA)
School of the Art Institute of Chicago (IL)
School of the Museum of Fine Arts (MA)
Vermont College of Fine Arts (VT)
Watkins College of Art, Design, & Film (TN)

You might even want to study 3D art and design abroad. Though international programs are not profiled in this book, some of the best are included in the following lists.

U.S. – ACCREDITED COLLEGES FOCUSED ON ART

International

Adelaide Central School of Art (Australia)

Alberta University of the Arts (Canada)

Bauhaus University Weimar (Germany)

Camberwell College of Arts (England)

Emily Carr Univ. of Art & Design (Canada)

Government College of Art & Craft (India)

Grekov Odessa Art School (Ukraine)

National Art School (Australia)

Nova Scotia College of Art & Design Univ. (Canada)

Ontario College of Art & Design Univ. (Canada)

Paris College of Art (France)

2021 QS RANKED TOP UNIVERSITIES FOR ART AND DESIGN WORLDWIDE

1. Royal College of Art (U.K.)
2. University of the Arts London (U.K.)
3. Parsons School of Design (NY-USA)
4. Rhode Island School of Design (RI-USA)
5. Massachusetts Institute of Technology (MA-USA)
6. Politecnico de Milano (Italy)
7. Aalto University (Finland)
8. School of the Art Institute of Chicago (IL-USA)
9. Glasgow School of Art (U.K.)
10. Pratt Institute (NY-USA)
11. ArtCenter (CA-USA)
12. Delft University of Technology (Netherlands)
13. Design Academy Eindhoven (Netherlands)
14. Tongji University (China)
15. Goldsmiths, University of London (U.K.)
16. Royal Melbourne Institute of Technology (Australia)
17. California Institute of the Arts (CA-USA)
18. Carnegie Mellon University (PA-USA)
19. Stanford University (CA-USA)
20. Hong Kong Polytechnic University (H.K. SAR)

Although this book only profiles a fraction of the art schools and only those U.S. colleges with bachelor's degree programs in sculpture, glass, and metal arts, there are undoubtedly many schools with excellent faculty and facilities, some even in your local area.

TOP 40 PROGRAMS IN JEWELRY AND METAL ARTS

California

Academy of Art University, SF – AA, BFA, MA, MFA – Jewelry & Metal Arts

California College of the Arts – BFA Jewelry & Metal Arts

Cal State Long Beach – BFA Metal & Jewelry

Humboldt State University -BFA Jewelry & Small Metals

San Diego State University – MFA Jewelry & Metalsmithing

Colorado

Colorado State University – BFA in Art, Metalsmithing

Georgia

Savannah Col. of Art & Design – BFA Jewelry Design, BFA Metals & Jewelry

Illinois

Illinois State University – BFA Wood & Metals

Northern Illinois University – BFA Metalwork, Jewelry Design, & Digital Fabrication

Southern Illinois University – BFA, MFA in Jewelry & Metalsmithing

Indiana

Ball State University - BFA in Art, focus in Metal

Indiana University at Bloomington – BFA Studio Art, focus - Metals + Jewelry

Kansas

University of Kansas – BFA Metalsmithing/Jewelry

Kentucky

Eastern Kentucky University – BFA Jewelry and Metals

Maine

Maine College of Art – BFA Metalsmithing/Jewelry

Michigan

Cranbrook Academy of Art – MFA Metalsmithing

Grand Valley State University – BFA Jewelry and Metalsmithing

Kendall College of Art & Design – BFA Metals and Jewelry Design

Univ. of Michigan, Ann Arbor – BFA Metalsmithing & Jewelry focus

Massachusetts

Mass. College of Art & Design – BFA Jewelry & Metalsmithing

New York

Fashion Inst. of Technology – AAS Jewelry Design

Rochester Inst. of Technology – BFA Studio Arts, Jewelry Design & Metalsmithing option

SUNY Buffalo – BFA Metals/Jewelry

SUNY New Paltz – BA/BFA Studio Arts in Metal

Syracuse University – BFA Studio Arts, emphasis in Jewelry & Metalsmithing

North Carolina

East Carolina University – BFA/MFA Metal Design

Ohio

Bowling Green State University - BFA, MFA focus Jewelry/Metal

Miami University – BFA Metals & Jewelry Design

University of Akron – BFA Jewelry & Metalsmithing

Oregon

University of Oregon – BFA Jewelry & Metalsmithing

Pennsylvania

Arcadia University – BFA in Art, concentration in Metals and Jewelry

Edinboro University – BFA/MFA Jewelry and Metalsmithing

Temple University – BFA in Metals/Jewelry/CAD-CAM

Rhode Island

Rhode Island School of Design – BFA Jewelry + Metalsmithing

Texas

Texas Tech – BFA in Art, emphasis in Jewelry Design & Metalsmithing

University of North Texas – BFA Metalsmithing & Jewelry

Virginia

Radford University – BFA Jewelry and Metalworking

Virginia Commonwealth University – BFA, MFA – Metal/Jewelry

Washington

Central Washington University – BA Art + Design, Studio Area - Jewelry/Metalsmithing

Wisconsin

University of Wisconsin, Milwaukee – BFA Jewelry & Metalsmithing

NON-BACHELOR'S DEGREE JEWELRY & METALSMITHING

American Jewelers Institute – Portland, OR – Bench jewelers program with classes in fabrication, mold construction, soldering, wax modeling, jewelry repair, and settings.

American School of Jewelry – Sunrise, FL - The Certified Master Jeweler Program - 1,650-hour program with training in precious metals, melting metals, wedding bands, ring sizing, stone setting, casting, and bezel design.

California Institute of Jewelry Training – Carmichael, CA - Certificate programs in jewelry repair, jewelry arts, and advanced metal techniques.

Conner Jewelers School – New Albany, IN – Training programs available in jewelry servicing, stone setting, wax modeling and casting, and the Jewelers of America Bench Certification.

Drouhard National Jewelers School – Mansfield, OH – Programs include jewelry repair, diamond setting, casting and production.

Gemological Institute of America (GIA) – Locations in London, UK; Bangkok, Thailand; Hong Kong; Mumbai, India; Surat, India; Taipei, Taiwan; Carlsbad, CA, USA; New York, NY, USA – Graduate Jeweler Program

Howard Academy for the Metal Arts – Stoughton, WI – Diploma program in metal arts with classes in fabrication, setting, shaping, soldering, riveting, plating, gemology, blacksmithing, mold making, and engraving.

Jewelry Arts & Design College – Los Angeles, CA – Programs include wax casting, fabrication, mounting, electroplating, gemology, metal arts, and jewelry design.

Miami Jewelry School – Miami, FL – Students can earn a diploma in jewelry technology, stone setting, and wax modeling and casting. Training includes melting, cleaning, filling, drilling, and soldering.

New Approach School for Jewelers – Franklin, TN – NASJ Graduate Bench Jeweler Program; CAD Academy, short and long classes with jewelry experts.

Revere Academy of Jewelry Arts – San Francisco, CA – Study fabrication, forging, gemology, metalsmithing, mold making, wax modeling, casting, repair, and settings.

Stewart's International School for Jewelers – Jupiter, FL – Programs include diamond setting, design and casting, and jewelry repair. Skills in soldering, casting, fabrication, stones, beads, sawing, drilling, and electroplating.

Studio Jewelers Ltd. – New York, NY – Training includes short and comprehensive courses in design, repair, settings, modeling, casting, stringing, and metals.

Texas Institute of Jewelry Technology – Paris, TX – Applied science degree program in Jewelry Technology through Paris Junior College.

TOP 20 COLLEGES FOR GLASS BLOWING

Alabama

University of South Alabama – BFA Studio Art, Glass

California

California College of the Arts – BFA Glass

Central College – BFA Glass Blowing

Florida

Jacksonville University – BFA Object Design (Glass)

Illinois

Illinois State University, BFA Studio Arts, focus in Glass

Southern Illinois University – BFA, MFA in Glass

Indiana

Ball State University – BFA in Art, focus in Glass

Louisiana

Tulane University – BFA Studio Art, discipline in Glass

Massachusetts

Massachusetts College of Art and Design – BFA, MFA in Glass

New York

Alfred University – the only ABET Accredited Glass Engineering program in the US

Hartwick College – BA in Art, focus in Glass

Rochester Institute of Technology – BFA Studio Art, Glass option; MFA Glass

Ohio

Bowling Green State University – BA/BFA/MFA in Studio Art, focus in Glass

Ohio State University – BA/BFA/MFA Studio Art, area - Glass

Rhode Island

Rhode Island School of Design – BFA/MFA Glass

Pennsylvania

Temple University – BFA/MFA in Glass

Texas

University of Texas, Arlington – BFA in Glass

Virginia

Virginia Commonwealth University – BFA, MFA – Glass

Washington

Washington

University of Washington – BA/MFA in Art - 3D4M Ceramics + Glass + Sculpture

Wisconsin

University of Wisconsin, Madison – BFA in Art, area Glass and Neon

ARTSY'S TOP 10 SCULPTORS TODAY

1. Jeff Koons – School of the Art Institute Chicago, Maryland Institute College of Art

2. Richard Serra – UC Berkeley, BA UCSB, BFA and MFA Yale University

3. Kiki Smith – did not graduate from college

4. Rachel Whiteread – Cyprus College of Art, MA University College, London Slade School of Art

5. Marc Quinn – Robin College, Cambridge

6. Tara Donovan – BFA Corcoran College of Art and Design, MFA Virginia Commonwealth University

7. Anish Kapoor – Hornsey College of Art, Chelsea School of Art and Design

8. Lynda Benglis – McNeese State University, BFA Newcomb College (Tulane University)

9. Antony Gormley – Trinity College, Cambridge, Saint Martin's School of Art, Goldsmiths, University College, London Slate School of Art

10. Damian Ortega – did not graduate from college

American Medallic Sculpture Association – American Medal of the Year Awards

2020 – Jeanne Stevens-Sollman – BSEd Rhode Island College, MFA Penn State

2019 – James Malonebeach – Masters in Art University of Iowa

2018 – Michael Meszaros – University of Melbourne (B.Arch.)

2016 – Susan Taylor – B.S. Wayne State University, MFA Cranbrook Academy of Art

2015 – Richard Bonham – Bachelors in Art Education at Kutztown State College

2014 – Michael Meszaros – University of Melbourne (B.Arch.)

DATA FOR CLASS OF 2026 (2025 IN YELLOW)

University	Total # Applied	Total Admit Rate	# Applied Regular Decision	# of Admits Regular	Reg. Dec. Admit Rate	Applied ED/SEA	Accepted Early Dec or SEA	ED/SEA Admit Rate
Brown	50,649	5.03%	44,503	1,651	3.71%	6,146	896	14.58%
Columbia	60,377	3.73%	54,072	1,603	2.96%	6,305	650	10.31%
Cornell	71,000	2,253%	61,500	3,922	6.7%	9,500	1,930	21.4%
Dartmouth	28,336	6.2%	25,703	1,237	4.81%	2,633	530	20.13%
Harvard	61,220	3.19%	51,814	1,214	2.34%	9,406	740	7.87%
Penn	55,000	4.4%	47,205	2,008	4.2%	7,795	1.218	15.63%
Princeton		3.98%	Princeton did not publish data for 2025 & will not publish data for 2026					
Yale	50,015	4.46%	42,727	1,434	3.36%	7,288	800	10.98%

University	Total # Applied	Total Admit Rate	Applied ED/Early Action	Accepted ED/Early Action	ED/EA Admit Rate
Boston College	40,477	16.5%	4,443	1,250	28.13%
Boston U	80,792	14.15%	6,311	1,640	25.99%
Duke	50,002	6.17%	4,015	855	21.3%
Emory	33,559	10.66%	2,127	672	31.59%
Georgetown	26,670	12.11%	8,832	881	9.98%
GWU	27,301	49%	1051	681	65%
Georgia Tech	50,601	17.14%	6,100	2,399	39.33%
Harvey Mudd	4,440	12.97%	Unavailable		
Johns Hopkins	37,100	6.49%	2,500	520	20.8%
MIT	33,976	3.94%	14,781	697	4.72%
NYU	105,000	12.2%	19,000	7,220	38%
Northeastern ED	91,100	6.7%	2,700	880	32.59%
Northeastern EA			50,000	3,000	6%
Northwestern	51,554	7.0%	26,506	1,675	12.87%
Notre Dame	26,506	12.87%	9,683	1,675	17.30%
Rice	31,424	8.56%	2,700	650	24.07%
Tufts	34,880	9.0%	Unavailable		
Tulane	42,000	10.0%	26,483	4,588	17.32%
USC	69,000	11.88%	USC does not have EA, ED, or REA		
Vanderbilt	46,717	6.13%	2,700	650	24.07%
Villanova	23,813	23.%	2025 – EA - 25.2%, ED – 58%		
Wash U St. L.	35,980	10.0%	Unavailable		17.6%
Wesleyan	14,521	13.86%	2026 – EDI - 44%, EDII – 31%		

UNIVERSITY OF CALIFORNIA

Based upon a *University of California Fact Sheet* from the University of California Office of the President, Graduate, Undergraduate, and Equity Affairs, Admissions, applyUC that says, "data subject to change", here is a comparison between admissions to the class of 2024 and admission to the class of 2026.

UNIVERSITY OF CALIFORNIA ADMISSIONS DATA				
University of California Campus	Residency of Applicants	Number of Applications		Acceptance Rate Class of 2026
		Class of 2024	Class of 2026	
Berkeley	California	50,223	72,417	14.5%
	Out-of-State	20,659	32,580	
	International	17,114	23,195	
	Total	88,026	128,192	
Davis	California	54,570	65,367	49.0%
	Out-of-State	6,505	10,748	
	International	15,798	18,610	
	Total	76,873	94,725	
Irvine	California	72,391	84,743	29.0%
	Out-of-State	8,000	14,309	
	International	17,525	20,113	
	Total	97,916	119,165	
Los Angeles	California	67,877	91,544	10.8%
	Out-of-State	23,016	34,627	
	International	17,944	23,608	
	Total	108,837	149,779	
Merced	California	22,244	22,516	87.6%
	Out-of-State	598	1,319	
	International	1,534	2,208	
	Total	24,376	26,043	
Riverside	California	43,151	46,456	65.8%
	Out-of-State	1,473	2,492	
	International	4,628	5,417	
	Total	49,252	54,365	
San Diego	California	66,350	84,326	34.3%
	Out-of-State	14,364	23,778	
	International	19,320	23,112	
	Total	100,034	131,226	
Santa Barbara	California	63,269	73,575	29.2%
	Out-of-State	10,988	18,432	
	International	16,690	18,984	
	Total	90,947	110,991	
Santa Cruz	California	43,893	53,051	58.8%
	Out-of-State	3,897	6,878	
	International	7,213	5,937	
	Total	55,003	65,886	

50

SPOTLIGHT ON 5 PROGRAMS

California College of the Arts (private, San Francisco, CA)

BFA Ceramics, Glass, Jewelry & Metal Arts, Sculpture

California College of the Arts offers 23 major programs in areas as diverse as comics, furniture, and textiles. Students are encouraged to take risks and explore different areas while also rigorously pursuing the mastery of their craft. Classes begin with the spirit of inquiry by blurring boundaries and then homing in on technique. Showcases offer a chance to view other's work. The Treadwell Ceramic Arts Center has a kiln, glaze room, personal student studios, and a 3D clay printer.

The glass program teaches glassblowing and flamework for hot glass, plaster and silicone molding, cold glass sculpting, and CAD modeling. In the jewelry and metal arts program, students learn rapid prototyping equipment including 3D printers, welders, and laser cutters. Students have the chance to intern with Bay Area metal artists. CCA's sculpture program takes an experimental approach to practice, performance, installation, and presentation using the latest in fabrication tools.

Massachusetts College of Art and Design

BFA Ceramics, Glass, Jewelry & Metalsmithing, Sculpture

MFA 3D Fine Arts

Students attend MassArt to focus their studies on art while gaining a broad background on the various forms and possibilities across the spectrum of media. Students begin with the Foundation Year gaining knowledge in art theory, history, design, and the technical aspects required for each concentration. Students take Liberal Arts courses that complement the material.

In 3D fine arts, students study clay, glass, metal, and wood. Renowned artists teach classes and guest artists share their wisdom. MassArt has excellent facilities to explore the field of your choice and collaborate with others along the way.

Rochester Institute of Technology (private, Rochester, NY)

BFA and MFA Ceramics, Glass, Metals and Jewelry Design, Sculpture

With 31 possible undergraduate degrees available in RIT's College of Art and Design, there are numerous program options. Students in the 3D programs learn spatial design, concept drawing, and art history. Students are not only taught their craft but also trained in the professional skills to run an arts business.

The ceramics program pottery wheel-throwing, hand-building, mold-making, glazing, firing, and material science. In the glass-focused degree, students learn glassblowing, flame-working, hot and kiln casting, cold-working, kiln-forming, glass imaging processes, and three-dimensional digital technologies. RIT's research focus emphasizes innovation, materials, and presentation.

The metals and jewelry design program focuses on aesthetics, materials, and advanced techniques. Materials include wood, clay, metal, and glass. RIT's sculpture program explores 3D elements of design with various materials, using techniques such as bronze casting, stone carving, steel fabrication, and mold-making.

Syracuse University (private, Syracuse, NY)

BFA in Ceramics, Jewelry and Metalsmithing, Sculpture, and Three Dimensional Studies
MFA Ceramics, Jewelry and Metalsmithing, Sculpture

SU's College of Arts and Sciences offers cutting-edge tools and opportunities in fine arts while SU's School of Visual and Performing Arts offers a focused BFA degree in illustration with skill-building in drawing, painting, digital media, and research. Students can focus on character development, editorial, sequential, and products. Meanwhile, students in the College of Arts and Sciences become grounded in hands-on training while gaining a liberal arts education at the same time. Syracuse also offers more than 100 study abroad programs in 60 countries, with short and long-term options. SU's London design program is excellent. However, SU also offers a MAYmester session in Museums and Contemporary Practices in New York City or Washington, D.C.

Virginia Commonwealth University

BFA Craft and Material Studies, Sculpture
MFA in Ceramics, Glassworking, Jewelry/Metalworking, Sculpture

VCUArts has 16 departments and programs. Students begin with the Art Foundation program (AFO) and are encouraged to discover their interests. The university facilitates students' expanded learning by funding research projects, internships, travel, and study abroad.

VCUArts' Craft and Material Studies program emphasizes the well-rounded exploration of art including clay, glass, fiber, metal, and wood. Students can choose classes in metal fabrication, pattern weaving, craft and digital technology, ceramics, furniture design, and hot glass fabrication.

THE MANY ROADS TO ARTISTIC SUCCESS

There are numerous ways you can be successful in 3D art and design. The training you get in college can be immensely valuable, particularly while being surrounded by highly skilled practitioners in the art. There is no one road to get to your goal, just as there is not one goal you may want to achieve. Thus, 3D art offers numerous pathways and byways. Some famous artists attended smaller programs where they gained a broader or more extensive liberal arts education. Others never went to college at all. Exposure to the many different forms of art with students who have diverse interests cannot be understated. Whichever road you take, enjoy the journey.

Two roads diverged in a wood, and I took the one less traveled by,
And that has made all the difference.

- Robert Frost

NEVER-ENDING FASCINATION

You will learn about history, culture, and psychology alongside design, materials, and artmaking. Your muses will lead you to unique opportunities. Furthermore, being seen in the throes of numerous excellent artists can be a big factor in the success of your projects. Securing materials, mitigating challenges, and working to obtain funding can be impediments or they can open new doors to partnerships. Experience makes a difference as young, talented, and eager neophytes seek to be recognized for their abilities in a field where longevity, respect, and reputation are often not acquired quickly.

The journey you are taking will have its ups and downs, but you will have stories to tell for the rest of your life. Your education may have unpredictable elements and pitfalls may lay in your path. Since you have endured a pandemic and the repercussions of a war, you are imbued with a few doses of resilience. Even so, you will be tested in art school as there is much to learn and a short amount of time.

You are embarking on a thrilling, demanding, and disciplined pursuit. You will work with extremely skilled and brilliant students who mastered drawing complex images when they entered elementary school. Some who have shown their art in galleries will blow you away with their abilities. However, rarely are art students equally skilled in all areas. Besides, some of your work in college may be collaborative where everyone contributes what they know. You will too.

You will find that some classmates will be amazingly talented. Do not let their abilities bring you down or make you feel as if you are not good enough. You will add your element and learn more during college. Besides, your enthusiasm for 3D art will show through in your work and effort. Recognizing your potential, commitment, and attitude, people will be awed at your creations as you also step back to appreciate your work.

Enjoy the experience.

Don't judge each day by the harvest you reap but by the seeds that you plant.

- Robert Louis Stevenson

CHAPTER 6

WHAT IS THE DIFFERENCE BETWEEN AN AA, AS, BA, BS, BFA, AND MFA?

"Give thanks for everything that happens to you, knowing that every step forward is a step toward achieving something bigger and better than your current situation."

— **Brian Tracy**

UNDERGRADUATE AND GRADUATE DEGREES

AA – Associate of Arts – 2-year degree

AS – Associate of Science – 2-year degree

BA – Bachelor of Arts – 4-year degree

BS – Bachelor of Science – 4-year degree

BFA – Bachelor of Fine Arts – 4-year degree with most classes focused on art

MFA – Master of Fine Arts – 1-2-year degree earned after the BA, BS, or BFA

Basically, BA and BS degrees are degrees that typically offer a liberal arts foundation along with a major or concentration in a specific subject. Meanwhile, a BFA is considered a professional arts-focused degree with fewer courses in English, science, math, social science, and the humanities. Thus, the BFA is a specialist qualification in the arts. A BA or BS degree in fine arts is also valuable. The BFA is more focused on the specific area of art you choose.

The BA and BS degrees include significantly more liberal arts classes and thus are more general degrees. However, the intention of the BFA degree is for students to pursue an arts-focused curriculum, and thus there are fewer general subject courses.

Finally, while many AA or AS degrees are focused on providing technical or professional skills, an AA or AS in these areas are often interchangeable. Similarly, a BA or BS in arts-oriented degrees are often interchangeable. However, a BFA may be seen as different since there is typically more coursework focused on your specific pursuit, and thus, you may have more technical experiences and knowledge than someone who has a BA or BS.

AA – ASSOCIATE OF ARTS

The Associate of Arts degree is typically a 2-year general studies degree offered online or in-person by a community college. However, some universities offer AA degrees as well. Often, the Associate of Arts degree focused on the liberal arts has no barrier to entry, meaning that students can enter most AA programs with a high school diploma or the equivalent. Some students take a longer or shorter time to complete the AA based upon their skills upon entering the program, certainty about the direction they are heading, and the transfer requirements for the program they desire. For example, students majoring in business may have additional business, communication, accounting, and economics requirements and need to create an academic plan early in their program to finish in two years.

AS – ASSOCIATE OF SCIENCE

The Associate of Science degree is very similar to the AA. However, the AS degree frequently emphasizes science and math and often has additional requirements.

BA – BACHELOR OF ARTS

The Bachelor of Arts degree is typically a 4-year degree offered online or in-person by a college or university. However, a few community colleges offer BA degrees as well. Some students complete their BA in fewer years depending upon AP/IB credit, dual enrollment in high school, and summer/intersession classes. College programs have stricter or less stringent requirements depending upon the school. The Bachelor of Arts degree frequently requires students to take lower-division (first and second year) liberal arts courses before taking specialized courses focused around a major or concentration in their third and fourth years.

The time required to earn a BA depends upon each student's skills and advanced placement credit when entering the program. Some students change the direction they are heading and their chosen major which can add more time. According to the National Center for Educational Statistics, college advisors aid students in finishing "on time" though less than half of all students in the United States who start a BA program finish their degree in four years.[1]

---

1   IEC NCES, "Digest of Education Statistics, Table 326.10," IES NCES, n.d., https://nces.ed.gov/programs/digest/d20/tables/dt20_326.10.asp?referer=raceindica.asp

BS – BACHELOR OF SCIENCE

The Bachelor of Science degree is very similar to the BA. However, the BS degree frequently emphasizes science and math and often has additional requirements.[2]

BFA – BACHELOR OF FINE ARTS

The Bachelor of Fine Arts is a 4-year college degree focusing on the arts. BFA students are often not required to take as many English, science, math, social science, and humanities courses. However, they must still complete roughly the same number of credits as a person who earns a BA or BS, and the courses are not necessarily easier. BFA students frequently take general art requirements to lay a foundation in drawing, graphic design, and courses in their specialty area during their first two years, along with basic writing and quantitative skill-building.

BFA students are traditionally art-in-practice students who learn the technical craft of their art form while putting in enormous numbers of hours practicing their skill doing assignments and participating in internships and experiential learning. Students who know that they want a future in the arts often finds this avenue perfectly tailored for their pursuits. However, students who change their minds and

---

2   IEC NCES, "Digest of Education Statistics, Table 326.10," IES NCES, n.d., https://nces.ed.gov/programs/digest/d20/tables/dt20_326.10.asp?referer=raceindica.asp

transfer to a university in another degree program may require an additional year to make up for coursework they have not completed.

MFA – MASTER OF FINE ARTS

The Master of Fine Arts is a graduate degree for students who have completed their BA, BS, or BFA. This degree takes one to two years depending upon the program, coursework, and experiential component, which may be a capstone, practicum, internship, or thesis. While there are also MA and MS degrees, many art students who continue their studies to earn a master's degree in the arts chose to focus on their field of interest. The MFA is an intensive immersion into a higher level of skill-building. However, students who graduate with an MFA have a broader range of talents and experiences than those who earn their bachelor's degree. While admission into these programs is generally selective, with planning, preparation, and a good portfolio, there are options for you to pursue your interests.

THE SEVEN MAJOR DIFFERENCES BETWEEN THE ASSOCIATE'S, BACHELOR'S, AND MASTER'S DEGREES

1. Starting Point
2. Academic Discipline
3. Time to Completion
4. Location of the Education
5. Educational Costs
6. Earning Power
7. Professional Opportunities

STARTING POINT

Most students who begin with an Associate of Arts (AA) or Associate of Science (AS) have no college credits. Starting from scratch with their college education, they accumulate their 60+ units beginning from this community college starting point. While most students earn AA or AS degrees at a community college, some earn this degree at a 4-year college or university.

The AA or AS is either a terminal degree, meaning that the student will not continue on with their bachelor's degree or just a steppingstone to their BA, BS, or BFA. The difference between the associate's and bachelor's degrees is just the starting point.

The starting point for students who pursue a bachelor's degree may be farther along the traditional 4-year pathway. Meanwhile, the starting point for the master's degree (MA, MS, or MFA) begins after obtaining a bachelor's degree.

ACADEMIC DISCIPLINE

Every degree encompasses different requirements. Requirements for the AA differ from an AS. Similarly, the requirements for the BA, BS, and BFA also differ. With two additional years of coursework, the BA, BS, and BFA are more thorough. The MA, MS, and MFA build upon the bachelor's degree and even deeper. Students studying painting will not take the same classes as those pursuing graphic design, though some may overlap. While both are essential to the fine arts, the necessary skills for each career area are distinct. Thus, the course requirements are also unique.

Furthermore, with the myriad of combinations, it is rare that any two undergraduate students have the same exact classes in the same exact order. Since the requirements for a chemistry degree are not the same as for biology

and painting differs from graphic design, the various degrees not only include a different number of credits but different types of classes and program specifications.

TIME TO COMPLETION

Associate of Arts (AA) and Associate of Science (AS) degrees typically take two years, while most BA, BS, and BFA degrees are 4-year programs, depending upon full-time or part-time status. Students who transfer credits into their program or earn credits by exam or experience can reduce their time to completion.

Some students may choose to extend their education in 3D art and design by earning a second bachelor's degree in another field. By cross-training in graphic design, photography, or marketing, students open more doors. Additionally, a degree in business on the bachelor's level or Master's in Business Administration (MBA) may lead to alternative leadership positions.

Time in college can be reduced. Some students enter a BA, BS, or BFA program having already completed college credits because they were dual-enrolled or they took college classes directly through a college or university ahead of time. Some students have taken AP/ IB tests from taking higher-level classes while in high school and earned qualifying scores to be granted credits by the college or university. Other ways students can enter at a different starting point are with credit-by-exam, CLEP tests, experiential credits, and those granted in the military.

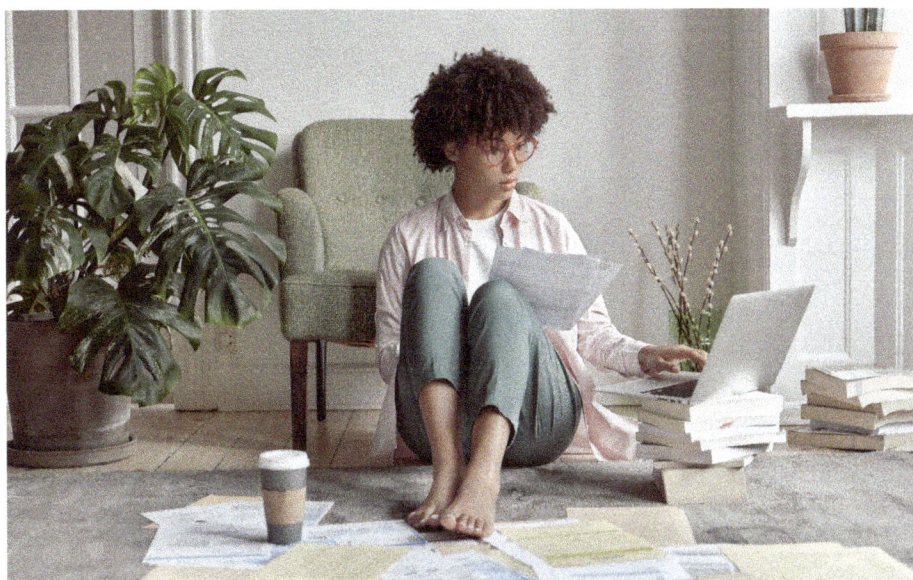

Colleges and universities are keenly aware of the challenges students face today with work, illness, and family responsibilities. Thus, many schools of higher education offer flexible enrollment with opportunities for part-time, evening, weekend, and online classes.

LOCATION OF THE EDUCATION

The AA and AS are earned at colleges that grant 2-year degrees. The location may be at a local community college or a university. BA, BS, and BFA programs are offered at a 4-year college or university. However, with online classes, students have the flexibility to take classes from colleges farther away as well. Thus, the location in which a typical student studies is not as set as it once was. Nevertheless, the in-person internships are often situated in corporate hubs and thus require grounding to a specific location.

EDUCATIONAL COSTS

Since the AA or AS requires a shorter amount of time and is typically completed at a lower-cost community college, the cost for an associate's degree is typically less than a bachelor's degree. Master's degree programs cost more per credit but take less time than a bachelor's degree.

On the other hand, many students can obtain financial aid in the form of grants, loans, and both merit and need-based scholarships. This aid can pay for school and reduce debt after college.

EARNING POWER

Students with more education can earn more. According to the 2019 National Center for Educational Statistics (NCES) average income data for the median person based on degree attainment,[3]

- Master's Degree or Higher - $70,000
- Bachelor's Degree - $55,700
- Associate's Degree - $43,300
- High School - $35,000

---

3   IES NCES, "Annual Earnings by Educational Attainment," IEC NCES, May 2021, https://nces.ed.gov/programs/coe/indicator/cba

Ofcourse, there is a wide range in annual salaries from those who have consistent work and are paid six-digit or seven-digit salaries to those who work one or two paid shows per year and earn less than $20,000. Thus, the average seems low when the variation is huge.

PROFESSIONAL OPPORTUNITIES

Earning a BA, BS, or BFA opens more doors than an AA or AS. Similarly, an MA, MS, or MFA opens more doors than a BA, BS, or BFA. Baccalaureate and master's degrees require more training. You can obtain this training through workshops or studio classes, but with a scholarship to pay for college, you might find that the training and opportunities are worth your time. Besides, you will gain additional skills that could prove valuable in your future.

It does not matter where you go and what you study,
what matters most is what you share with yourself and the world.

— **Santosh Kalwar**

CHAPTER 7

COLLEGE ADMISSIONS: TERMS, DATA, APPLICATIONS, TESTS, AND ESSAYS

"Our heads are round so thought can change direction."

– Francis Picabia

A pply to the colleges that have the curriculum, clubs, activities, and opportunities that fit your interests the best. Some colleges stand out for 3D art and design with amazing faculty, excellent facilities, and relatively easy access to job opportunities. While most students consider New York City, Los Angeles, Chicago, and San Francisco locations for internships, they should not discount other metropolitan areas around the country that are meccas for art and design.

Planning is required before you apply. Let's look at a few terms you should know, then move on to community service, connecting with the colleges, and whether or not you should take standardized tests. Then, I offer some data, a checklist, and some tips for applying to and succeeding in college. Best wishes on your journey!!!

ADMISSIONS TERMS TO KNOW

Admissions Tests – These are tests like SAT, ACT, GMAT, GRE, MCAT, etc. that universities use to standardize student's aptitude in foundational academic skill areas.

Admit Rate – The percent of applicants who are admitted.

Articulation Agreement – This is the agreement between 2-year and 4-year colleges that determines whether credits transfer from one institution to another.

Candidate Reply Date – For freshman admissions, students must reply back to colleges by May 1 with their choice of college or university they will attend from those in which they were accepted.

Class Rank – Most high schools no longer rank students. However, a few still do. This ranking puts students in order of weighted GPA. Some schools rank in percentiles or deciles.

Coalition Application – This standardized application app can be sent to multiple schools within the network of approximately 150 colleges. Most colleges also require supplemental applications with additional essays and requirements.

College Credit – Most colleges require 120 – 130 semester credits to graduate with a bachelor's degree. Students earn credits upon successful completion of classes. Colleges may award college credit for qualifying AP/IB scores, CLEP exams, and military training courses.

Common Application – This is a standardized application app that can be sent to multiple schools within the network of approximately 900 colleges. Most colleges also require supplemental applications with additional essays and requirements.

Deferred Admission – After the EA/ED admissions cycle, students are accepted, denied, or deferred to regular decision. Typically, the chances of being accepted during the regular admissions cycle after being deferred is 5–10%.

Deferred Enrollment – Colleges allow a student to postpone their attendance for up to one year. Note: Not all colleges allow students to defer.

Domestic Student – Students who are U.S. residents no matter where they live. Some schools reserve this term for U.S. citizens who are out-of-state students.

Early Action (EA) – An early application submission in which a student also finds out their decision before regular decisions. Early action is not binding, meaning that students do not need to enroll if accepted. Most EA application due dates are between October 15th and November 15th. Almost all EA decisions come back between December 1st and February 1st with most responses between December 10th – 20th.

Early Decision (ED) – A few colleges have ED whereby a student commits to one school should they be accepted. Students agree to attend when they apply, and they can only apply to one ED school. If admitted, students pay the deposit and withdraw their applications from other schools. ED applications are typically due November 1 and decisions typically come back in mid-December.

Financial Aid – This is money given to help pay for school and can be composed of scholarships, grants, loans, and work-study. Financial aid may be granted from the government, college, or private organizations.

First-Generation – Students are 'first-gen' if neither of their parents has a four-year college degree. Some states differ and say that the parents of first-gen students never attended college.

High School GPA – This number is recalculated differently by each college depending upon whether they include 9th – 11th, summers, middle school, AP/IB/Honors credit, and courses like health, computer applications, leadership, sports, etc. Some colleges like the University of California cap their weighted GPA for admissions purposes with only 8 semesters of 'honors' points. No more than 4 of these can be from 10th grade.

In-State – These students are students who have residency in the state (driver's license, taxes, etc.) no matter where they physically live.

International – These applicants are not residents of the United States in the eyes of admissions. For some students, this designation varies from state to state.

Legacy – A child with a close relative who graduated from a given college. Some colleges give preference to legacy applicants.

Lower Division – These are courses typically taken in your first two years of college. Most community college classes are lower division. At a university, lower division courses for a BA or BS degree are primarily liberal arts classes.

Need-Aware Admissions – The policy where admissions teams consider financial circumstances in the admissions process.

Need-Blind Admissions – The policy where admissions teams do not consider financial circumstances in the admissions process.

Open Admissions – A college opens enrollment to all students until the seats are filled without consideration of past academic performance.

Placement Tests – Most colleges require certain levels of mastery before entering a class. Upon enrolling in a college, students take placement tests to determine the level in which they are placed. Since information recall may not be strong from a class taken years before, you should review the material before you take the test or you may need to take one or two additional remedial classes which may prolong graduation.

Portal – This is the online center where you log in to determine what the college is missing (transcripts, test scores, portfolio, etc.), scholarships, and your admissions status.

Registrar's Office – This is the office of college officials who are responsible for your student records - recording grades, certifying completion, and sending transcripts.

Residency – This is the determination of state residency, non-resident U.S., or international.

Rolling Admission – This is the college policy to accept students as the applications come into the school rather than waiting for a specific date. Many colleges with rolling admissions will determine your admission to the school within a month of receipt of your materials.

Summer Melt – The phenomenon whereby students submit an intent to enroll at a college after being admitted, pay the deposit, and decide not to attend during the summer. While this situation may have increased during the pandemic, the phenomenon has recurred for decades. The primary reasons for summer melt include the inability to pay, illness, family matter, change of heart, acceptance of a job, or getting off the waitlist at another college.

Transfer Student – A student who has taken college classes after completing high school and applies to a 4-year university. Typically, college classes taken during high school still allow students to apply for freshman admissions.

Upper Division – These are courses typically taken in your second two years of college. At a university, upper division courses for a BA or BS degree are primarily major-specific classes.

Waitlist – Admissions offices accept, deny, or waitlist students. Those students on a waitlist must wait until a spot opens. If there is a vacancy, the student may be taken off of the waitlist on a priority basis, ranking system, or admissions review.

Yield – This is the percent of admitted students who pay the deposit with the intent to enroll (enrolled/admitted x 100).

PRESIDENT'S VOLUNTEER SERVICE AWARD

Many students support their communities through service opportunities. These include volunteering in homeless shelters, soup kitchens, schools, sports camps, research, nursing homes, Special Olympics, Adopt-a-Family, Habitat for Humanity, Youth Action Teams, political campaigns, docent work at theatres, charity 5Ks, concerts, parades, international projects, medical missions, church-sponsored service work, and forest, park, beach, and wetlands cleanups. Some students are recognized for their work with certificates others just serve to help society. Either way, by accumulating hours, you can earn one of these Presidential Volunteer Service Awards.

Community service demonstrates your commitment to those around you while also giving you a deeper understanding of societal challenges. While there are no easy answers, serving at food banks, libraries, science centers, and recycling locations can help you ponder solutions.

Hours Required to Earn Awards in Each Age Group

Age Group	Bronze	Silver	Gold	Lifetime Achievement Award
Kids (5–10 years old)	26–49 hours	50–74 hours	75+ hours	4,000+ hours
Teens (11–15)	50–74 hours	75–99 hours	100+ hours	4,000+ hours
Young Adults (16–25)	100–174 hours	175–249 hours	250+ hours	4,000+ hours
Adults (26+)	100–249 hours	250–499 hours	500+ hours	4,000+ hours

COLLEGE ADMISSIONS:

Success in the Face of Uncertainty

There are no guarantees in college admissions. However, planning is essential for success. The most beneficial advice is to pursue your passions with gusto, train to be the best you can be, take advantage of internships and experiences, and meet lots of people along the way.

Remember, "life is a journey, not a destination." Often the journey is more exciting, leading to lessons, friendships, and unforgettable moments. However, the fact is, in the end, if college is your goal, then you need to know a few action items to remember for success.

Should you worry about grades? Of course. You should also take classes that will challenge you. Colleges pick the best candidates from those who apply. Students must be academically prepared, socially conscious, and talented in a few different areas in which they are passionate (design, graphic arts, musical instruments, theatre, debate, public speaking, leadership, athletics, community service, computer coding, robotics, construction, etc.).

The college selection process is not that much different than companies picking employees. While colleges are more or less competitive, companies may have only one job, and a hundred resumes. Discover the unique drive and internal motivations within you that make you the very best you can be. Be exceptional at what you choose to do academically, personally, and professionally.

Most of all, You Do You!

TALENT FOCUSED

Not all schools require high grades and test scores. Many are simply interested in selecting students who are the most talented, most driven, and the most willing to be team players on the college campus. Thus, you should take a solid set of courses and fulfill the standard requirements.

Hundreds of thousands of students attend college with GPAs between 2.5 and 3.5. Furthermore, most college students today, more than ten million never take standardized tests. If you are applying to highly competitive schools, you should take the test. However, there are hundreds of colleges that do not require test scores in 2022 and probably never will in the future.

In a comprehensive April 22, 2022, report,[1] Melanie Hanson of the Education Data Initiative did a fabulous job presenting copious educational data. I pulled some that you may find informative.

In 2020, total college enrollment was approximately 19 million, dropping by two million from its high in 2010 with 3.1 million in graduate school. Approximately one-third (66.2%) of high school students go on for post-secondary study. California has the most college students with 2.72 million; 89.5% attend public institutions; 11.6% leave the state to attend college; 35.8% of fulltime college students are female.

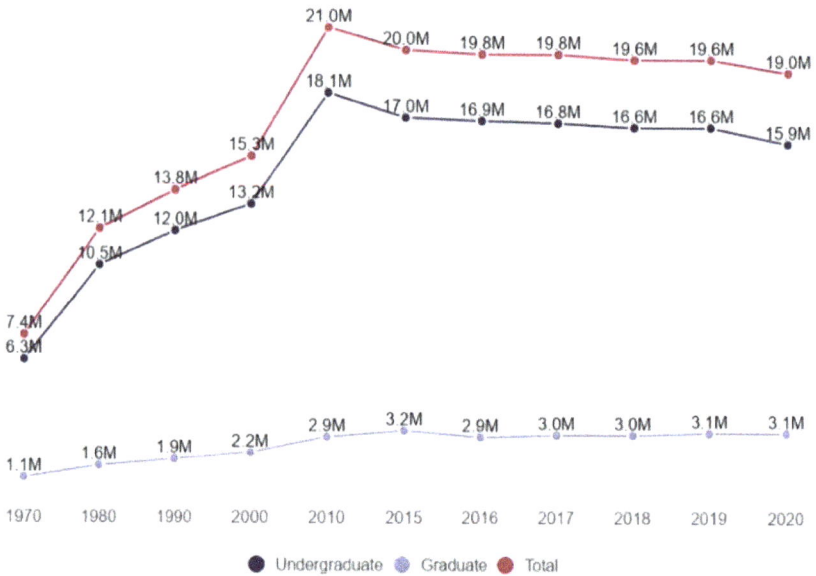

In approximate numbers, here is some college student data.

DEMOGRAPHIC CHARACTERISTICS

Caucasian – 54.3%
LatinX - 19.3%
Black or African American - 12.6%

Asian or Asian American – 6.8%
American Indian/Alaska Native – 0.66%%
Pacific Islander – 0.26%

1   Melanie Hanson. "College Enrollment & Student Demographic Statistics" EducationData.org, April 22, 2022, https://educationdata.org/college-enrollment-statistics

Foreign-born – 12%

Women - 55.5%

15 years old or younger – 0.7%

Under 24 years old – 92%

45 years old or older – 1.5%

DEGREES AND MAJORS

4.43 million students graduated in 2021

* 24.6% received associate's degrees

* 49.9% received bachelor's degrees

* 20.8% earned master's degrees

* 4.7% earned doctorates/professional degrees

Majors – 58% of all bachelor's degrees are in five areas of study

* 19.1% in business

* 11.9% in health-related professions

* 8% social sciences and history

* 5.9% in psychology

* 5.9% in biological and biomedical sciences

COMPETITIVE COLLEGE ADMISSIONS

A few highly selective colleges seek extraordinary talent over academics, but most zero in on a student's challenging courses and high grades. To gain admission into the most highly selective academic colleges, you must take the most challenging course load you can manage and succeed. Highly selective colleges want disciplined scholars AND remarkably talented students.

Determine what you can handle, knowing that some colleges with extremely competitive admission will only take students who have completed more than ten AP, IB, or honors classes over the four years.

Why would the most competitive colleges require classes like AP Calculus or Physics for an art program? However daunting these classes may seem, remember, the top colleges have lots of applicants, and they need to draw the line somewhere. UCLA had 149,779 applicants for fall 2022; UC Berkeley had 128,192 applicants. The numbers are truly staggering since neither first-year class will have no more than 7,000 students starting in the fall.

College admissions can feel like a rollercoaster of energy and emotion. Creating a portfolio of talent, training, and experience is just the beginning. Meanwhile, some colleges want to see standardized test scores aided by practice. Applications and essays may seem easy at first, but managing the various requirements and deadlines can be difficult. Therefore, this moment is a good time to get a calendar and organize your tasks.

REQUEST INFORMATION

Almost every college has a location, a link, or a contact us page where you can request information from the school. If you are considering a school, request information from them. In this way, they may send you updates, scholarship opportunities, a valuable application fee waiver, special invites, and other

information that could be valuable in the process. Of course, you may not need one more e-mail, and you may be receiving e-mails from the school anyway. Still, I recommend that you fill out their form. Then, since you are likely to be inundated with e-mails, make a file folder in your e-mail for all colleges you are considering. Then, when you get an e-mail from one of those schools, file it away.

STANDARDIZED TESTING

A few schools still require standardized testing. Check first. Many colleges are test-optional. This means that you are not required to take the SAT or ACT. However, if you have a good score, it may make all the difference in gaining admission. College admissions offices are studying this topic and considering their future policies. Much of their concern began with test cancelations worldwide due to the pandemic.

Schools did not want to let students into their site to take the test who may be infected, nor were they able to ensure safety. In addition, social distancing requirements limited the number of students who could take a test at any given site. Yet, for decades, college admissions decisions centered around grades and test scores. This change in the landscape of decision-making has rattled admissions departments.

Meanwhile, some colleges proclaim that test-optional truly means that the test is not required. Yet, evidence proves otherwise. Thus, many students are still

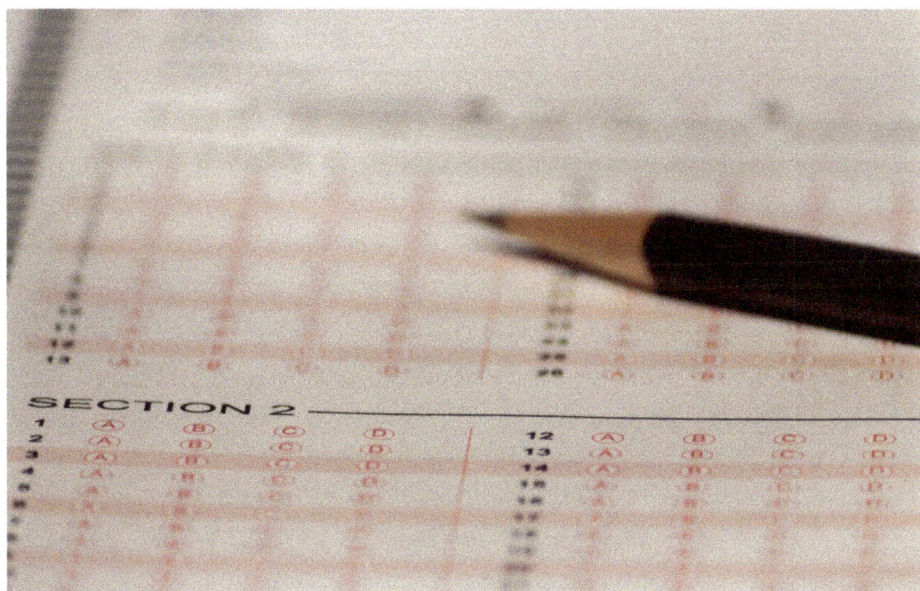

taking the test and working around the hurdles amid the confusion. Competition continues to drive students to present evidence to show that they are worthy candidates. In the end, colleges need to make a final decision between very good candidates. If one student has a high score, that student may have a higher likelihood of admission depending upon the admissions committee's decision-making process.

Data show that students who submitted scores within the college's range or higher were accepted at a higher rate than those without a score. Some schools are test blind. While they claim not to consider your scores, a few of these colleges still provide a place to input your scores. Thus, they are not truly blind. Nevertheless, the decision regarding whether you take the test or submit the score is yours. If the school does not require an admissions test, you can choose to take the test and submit it as you like. If your academics are solid and you are willing to prepare for the test, you should take the test.

APPLYING EARLY
Early Action (EA), Restricted Early Action (REA), and Early Decision (ED)

With low acceptance rates, the chance to get more scholarship money, and the chaos surrounding the cancellations and changes in AP, IB, SAT, and ACT testing, students clamor to apply early to schools. In addition, applications to the top schools increased during the pandemic, resulting in colleges needing to make difficult admissions decisions in their quest to build a diverse, talented, and engaged class of students. Furthermore, students applying early have access to many more scholarship options. This confluence sent students in droves to apply early. This trend is likely to continue.

In Early Action (EA), Restricted Early Action (REA), and Early Decision (ED), students apply in late summer or early fall to college and generally find out around winter break, though some decisions come out earlier and a few arrive later. This advantage not only gives students a chance for more scholarship money in some cases but the benefit of finding out early reduces the tension of the long waiting period to find out about Regular Decision schools.

Early Action (EA) and Restricted Early Action (REA) are different. In restricted early action, a limitation is placed on either how many or what colleges you can apply to simultaneously. Many REA schools do not allow students to apply to other

early action schools, though some will allow students to apply early to public colleges. Check the colleges to be sure. In addition, some schools like Georgetown will allow students to apply EA elsewhere but not apply to a binding Early Decision (ED) program where the student commits to attending if they are accepted. However, most EA schools do not have these restrictions, and some students apply to a handful of EA schools during the admissions process.

Early Decision (ED) is a binding agreement between the student and college with signatures from the student's parents and the high school assuring that the student is committed and will attend. Each of these parties acknowledges and agrees that, if granted admission, they will fulfill their agreement. There are caveats to this, though you should go into the agreement fully committing to your ED school.

There are incentives to applying ED. Frequently, acceptance rates are higher. Also, at some schools, a large percentage of their class is filled with students who profess their unequivocal love for their dream school. Students who know they have a top choice school, have the necessary admissions prerequisites fulfilled, and are committed to accepting the binding agreement to attend, should apply ED.

COMMON APPLICATION, COALITION APPLICATION, OR COLLEGE-SPECIFIC APPLICATION

Every college's process is unique. However, there are a few commonalities. In 2022, approximately 900 colleges used the Common App; about 150 colleges used the Coalition Application. A few used both. The University of California system has its own application as do the California State Universities and the Texas schools.

The Common App and Coalition App may be started early. In your junior year, consider getting a head start on reviewing what is required. The college-specific questions may change each year. However, the basic application is generally the same and can be created ahead of time. At the end of July, make a copy of everything you have completed just in case.

Some schools admit on a rolling basis. 'Rolling' means that periodically, after all of the materials are received, the admissions committee determines who they will accept, and they send the notification right away. Some students are accepted as early as August. The thrill of acceptance cannot be overstated.

ESSAYS

The Common Application and Coalition essays are often posted months ahead of time. Since this main essay is required or recommended for nearly all Common Application and Coalition Application schools, this is an excellent place to start thinking about what you might want to say to colleges.

In addition to the main essay on the Common Application and Coalition Application, about three-fours of the colleges have their own specific questions or essays. In August, most admissions applications are open and ready for you to dive into the college-specific questions, though many of the essay topics are available earlier, and some schools hold out until later for their big essay reveal.

These can be prepared ahead of time too. One popular question is, "What activity is most important to you and why?" Another is "Why did you choose your major?" A third common question is, "Why do you want to attend our school?" For others, you should prepare or at least consider the topics of diversity, adversity, and challenges since these topics have become increasingly important in the admissions process. Everyone has a challenge they needed to overcome. What did you learn from that experience?

Complete the application fully. Think carefully about optional sections. Typically, universities offer you the chance to provide the school with just the right cherry on top of the sundae, allowing you to share something unique about you. If you have absolutely nothing to say, leave it blank. There is an additional information section on the main Common App, Coalition Application, and University of California application. This location is not a place to write another essay, but you can include information that cannot be adequately explained in the rest of the application.

There are also schools that include scholarship essays within the supplement part of the application. Start early.

LETTERS OF RECOMMENDATION

Most colleges on the Common App and Coalition App, though not all, request letters of recommendation from a counselor and one or more teachers. For engineering programs, university admissions offices may want academic teachers in mathematics, science, or humanities. Plan for this. Occasionally, there is often a section for optional recommendations too. In this location, you might get a recommendation from a summer program leader or someone with whom you did an internship. If you were in a sport, there is a location for a coach on about a quarter of the applications. Finally, if there is a supplemental application where you can show your talent, projects, writing, or art, for example, on SlideRoom, they often require separate recommendations reviewed by the specific program.

COLLEGE APPLICATION CHECKLIST

☐ Calendar - Keep a calendar of due dates for summer program applications, contests, AP tests, SAT/ACT, applications, scholarships, and financial aid.

☐ Career Interest Survey - Take a career interest/aptitude test. Learn more about the majors and career options that best fit your interests and abilities

☐ Consider College Majors – What classes are offered in the curriculum? Many students who dislike math are surprised to learn that most business degrees require both calculus and statistics while incorporating math in nearly every class. It pays to research the subjects now.

☐ Investigate Colleges – Consider possible schools based on the programs they offer, research opportunities, internships, clubs, activities, sports, and personal interests - visit if possible.

☐ National College Fair – In the spring, colleges send representatives to a couple of dozen cities where you can meet with their admissions staff. These are good to walk around and learn more about the colleges and ask questions.

☐ Request Information – Fill out the request for information for each college you are considering so that they keep you informed of opportunities you may not have considered. They may send you a fee waiver or streamlined application.

☐ Summer Programs – Summer camps, skill-building, tours, research, internships, and college programs often have deadlines. Apply and consider your options.

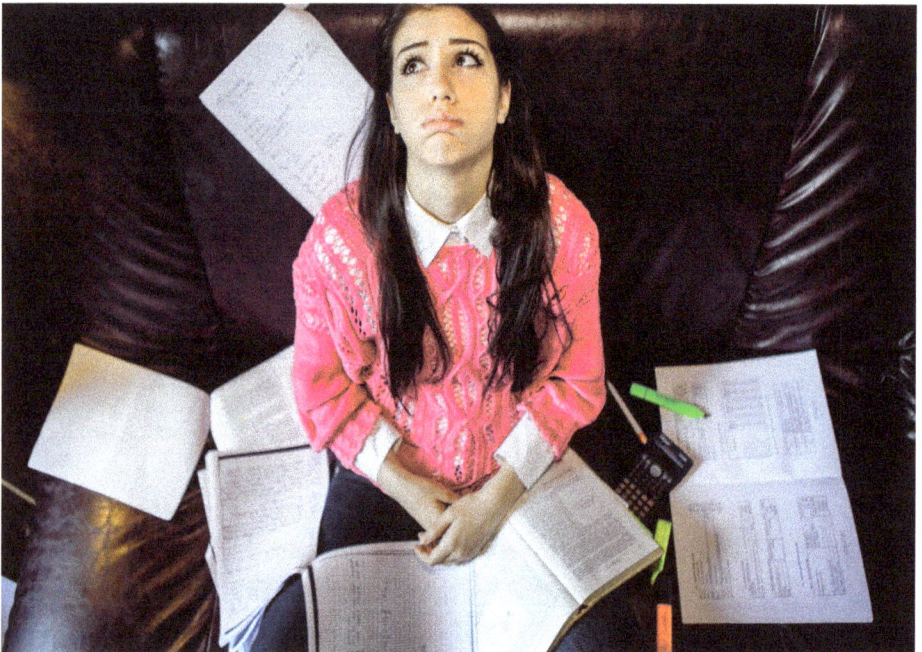

- ☐ **Narrow Choices** – Narrow down your choices in the summer before your senior year so that you have an equal number of target, reach, and safeties.

- ☐ **Communicate With Your Counselor** – Your counselor is your guide who not only helps you with your course selection but also advocates for you in the admissions process through their recommendation and sometimes with admissions. Get to know them.

- ☐ **SAT/ACT** – Decide if there is a benefit of taking these tests for the colleges you are considering.

- ☐ **Extended Time** – Determine if you qualify for extended time on tests.

- ☐ **Fee Waivers** – Ask your counselor if you qualify for fee waivers for the SAT/ACT, CSS Profile, or application fees.

- ☐ **Resume** – Create a resume whether or not the college requests one – some do. First, you may need one for a job. However, a resume allows you to gather your activities and accomplishments in one place for you to see what you want to present to a school.

- ☐ **Essays and Short Answer Questions** – Determine aspects of your life that stand out. Give colleges the best impression of your interests, inspirations, commitment, and life journey.

- ☐ **Counselor Recommendation Form** – Determine if your school requires a special form to obtain a counselor recommendation.

- ☐ **Recommendations** – Ask your teachers in the spring of your junior year or when school starts in your senior year.

- ☐ **Early Action/Early Decision** – These applications are due first, typically between October 15th and November 15th.

- ☐ **Regional Representative** – Some colleges have a regional representative. If you have any specifications, contact them to have them answer questions you cannot find the answers to on the website.

- ☐ **Transcripts** – Order transcripts to be sent to colleges from your high school (s) and any colleges you have attended. Note: Some colleges like the University of California do not want transcripts sent until you are admitted.

- ☐ **Deadlines** – Keep your eye on the deadlines.

- ☐ **Portals** – You must log into your portal after you submit your application and then every couple of weeks afterward to see if the college is missing something from your file. Some colleges will close your application if you do not log in or will move your early application to regular decision.

- ☐ **Scholarships** – Scholarships vary in due dates. Some begin the process of considering students in the spring of your junior year. The Coca-Cola Scholarship is due October 31st. However, due dates continue throughout most of your senior year. Scan www.fastweb.com and www.bigfuture.collegeboard.org/scholarship-search.

- ☐ **Regular Decision** – Regular decision applications for public colleges vary, but many are right after Thanksgiving. Regular decision application deadlines for most private schools are the first two weeks of January.

- ☐ **FAFSA** – Apply for federal financial aid (grants, work study, and loans).

- ☐ **CSS Profile** – About 300 colleges require this form to obtain financial aid.

- ☐ **Student Aid Report (SAR)** – Approximately 4 weeks after completing your FAFSA you should receive your SAR. Follow the instructions to complete updates or add schools.

- ☐ **Update Colleges** – Make sure you update colleges with your continued interest.

- ☐ **Keep Copies** – Keep copies of your application materials in a folder.

- ☐ **Visit Colleges** – If possible, visit colleges to which you were accepted. Since you are going to live there for four years, you should get a feel for the campus and not just judge a school by its rankings.

- ☐ **Communicate With Students** – Find students who currently attend the university who are willing to answer a few questions. How hard is it to change your major? Are students friendly? What do students do on the weekends? Ask your counselor, teachers, or the admissions office if they can refer you to a student who currently attends or just graduated.

- ☐ **Waitlisted Schools** – Most schools will allow you to write a letter updating them on your accomplishments during your senior year and your continued interest. Read the instructions since every school has a different format and set of requirements. Demonstrate your commitment.

- ☐ **Candidate Reply Date** – By May 1st you must choose one school and place a deposit.

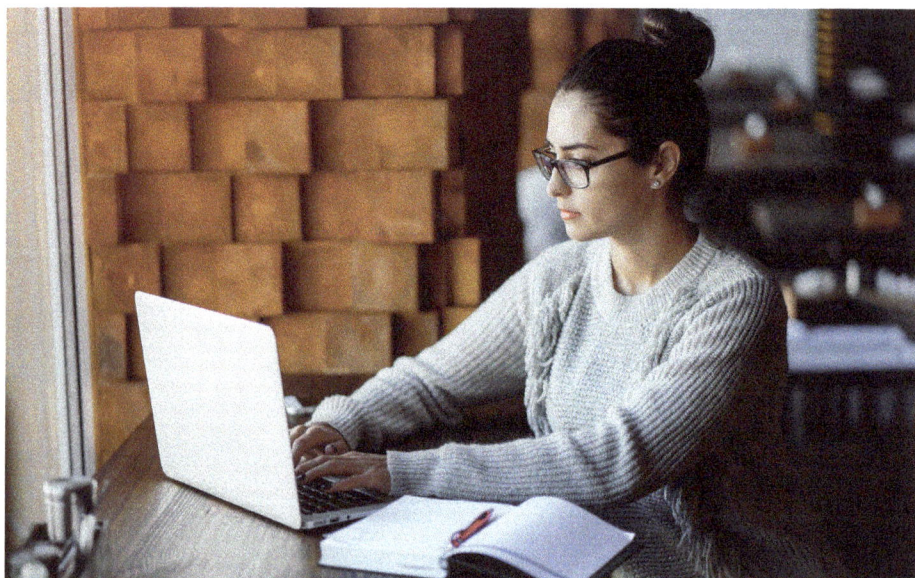

☐ Senior Year Grades – Colleges rescind admissions offers for students who do poorly in their senior year. Do not slack off. You will regret it.

DECISIONS, DECISIONS: WAITING FOR A RESPONSE

The period between submitting your application and getting your admissions results may not require a tremendous amount of work, but it does require patience and diligence. First, most schools will send you a link to a portal where you will check your results, though the most important reason for checking every couple of weeks is to ensure that the college is not missing something or has not offered you the chance to apply for an extra scholarship.

Check your portal regularly. Otherwise, read the college's correspondence sent through your e-mail. Waiting is difficult. These few months are a tough period because students want to know. However, the college typically lists the date they will send out the results on the portal. Other popular sites post their decision notification dates too. You will find out soon.

THICK OR THIN ENVELOPE

Students clamor for the mail each spring waiting to hear via e-mail, the college portal, or the mail - welcome packet or denial letter. You know spring has come as regular decision admissions results steadily roll, one at a time. In March, every day seems to last 26 hours, two extra for the period that lingers until that day's announcement. With each school announcing on a different day, the slow drip torture waiting to find out is exacerbated by the uncanny way each college picks a different day in March to announce their decision.

At some point you will know. That statement seems like little solace in the middle of the fray. You have until May 1 to make a decision, though with limited housing available and a first-come, first-served basis of selection, the pressure is on to choose. Even so, visiting the college is vital, despite the fact that AP tests and finals are just around the corner and there seems like there is no time. However, this decision influences where you will live, eat, study, make friends, take classes, and get involved for four years. If you do not consider your options, you are basing your decision on a few college-selected pictures and the tweets or feeds of other people.

There are many variables to consider in the end. This is why forward thinking at the beginning of the application process is valuable and even necessary to seek scholarships, merit money, or opportunities for financial aid. This proactive planning is especially needed with the spike in college applications at selective schools and the ever-changing landscape of test-optional admissions. MIT, for example, resumed its test requirement.

Plan ahead. The college application process is not a good time to procrastinate. The fall of your senior year is tough, often with a demanding course load. It is even tougher for athletes who compete in a fall sport. However, throughout your life you will need to work on time management, organization, and goal setting. This is a good time to start so you do not miss thousands of dollars in financial aid. Time management challenged students who adjusted their lifestyles due the self-paced and online classes and assignments during the pandemic.

CELEBRATING ACCEPTANCES AND DEALING WITH REJECTION

Acceptance is not guaranteed. The probabilities are low at the most highly selective schools. However, you just need to work hard in school to have what it takes and give this commitment to academics all you have. When you find out the results, you will celebrate your acceptances.

Congratulations! The colleges in which you gain admission go on your list of wins. Check your financial aid and scholarship packages too. Money is often an important factor in making your decision. Consider visiting the school. Many students apply to college merely by someone's recommendation, *U.S. News and*

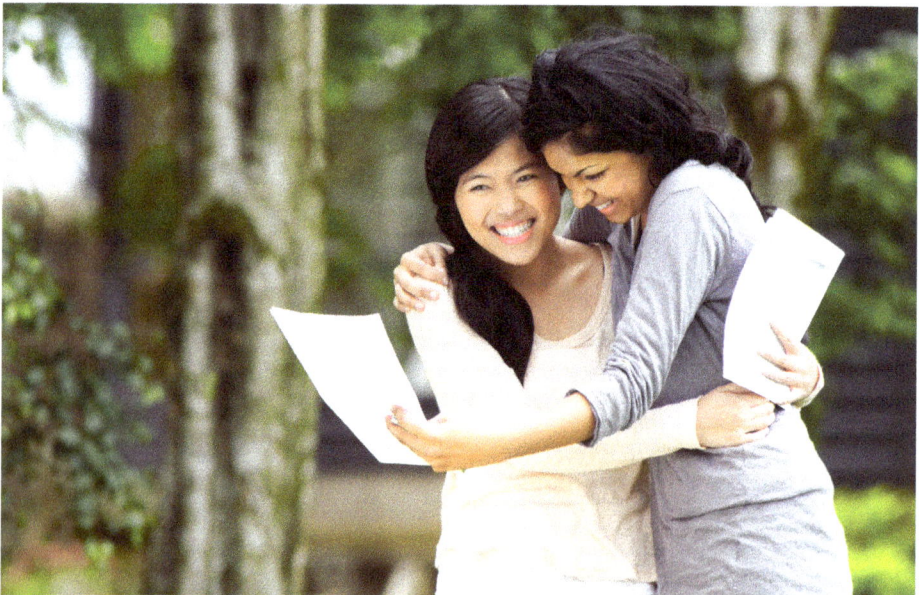

World Report ranking, looking at campus photos on Google, or researching profiles posted on a website or in a book.

There is nothing that replaces the actual campus visit. After all, you will be spending a few years there. While you may not be accepted everywhere you apply, you may decide when you visit that the college is high on your list or that you do not want to apply after all. Understandably, the pandemic's uncertainty added more question marks to an already complicated set of admissions processes.

The buzzword for 2020-2030 is resilience. It is never easy to be rejected. However, rejection happens, and you will survive this. Note that many colleges still accept applications in April, May, and June long after most school's applications are closed. Look up those colleges if you did not get accepted or if you want to see what other schools might be good options for you. In April and May, Google "College Openings Update". You will be surprised to see the colleges that show up on the list that still have open spots.

WAITLISTS: THE ART OF WAITING

Immediately confirm if you are given a waitlist spot and still want to attend. There is often a deadline. You do not want to miss this. If you are no longer interested or have selected another school, go into the portal and turn down the offer. Someone else is bound to be thrilled by your anonymous gift.

If you are still interested, find the location on the portal or site designated by the college to update them on what you have done – accomplishments, awards, extra class, honors, art, shows, or films. You only want to add what they have not yet seen, but if you have taken the initiative to do something more than what you originally stated on the application, by all means, tell them.

You could just wait for their decision, but you are better off being proactive and showing that you really want to be at their school. Students do get off the waitlists at most schools. How much do you want to attend? Meanwhile, you will have to deposit somewhere else before the May 1st deadline. Stay hopeful. This next year will be a significant step along your journey. Relax!

ACCEPTANCE IS JUST THE BEGINNING

Once you are accepted to college, you begin your journey toward your future. They call graduation "commencement" because you start your trek on your own path. The decisions you make now are primarily yours with significantly less input from your parents. For better or worse, your parents taught you lessons that you will keep or discard. Now, your behaviors, attitudes, internships, study abroad, and career choices will determine what you become.

Warning ahead of time…the path is rarely straight and there are pitfalls along the way. Much like Monopoly, you will roll the dice and move ahead a few squares, but you will go back a few spaces as well. You might buy a house. You might collect some cash; you might lose some too. Life is full of lessons. Successful adults can sometimes look back and forget about the wrong turns because they sting at the time and then they are dismissed over the years as lessons.

I have literally been in college for nearly fifty years and have degrees that span a multitude of disciplines. I have also taught chemistry, mathematics, engineering, counseling, public relations, and politics. Here are twenty-one tips as you go forward.

1. Attend class even when other students don't. Surprisingly, many lecture halls are half empty when there isn't a test. Go anyway. Most college professors know if you attend.

2. Buy your books and start reading before the semester starts. When classes begin, you live in a blizzard of activities, opportunities, and assignments. Again, surprisingly, most students do not complete their assigned readings. Some get by without reading but getting As that way is tough.

3. Work ahead. Finish your paper or project first, then go out and celebrate your friend's birthday, sports team win, or friend-group's successes. Not only can you be more relaxed, but you might even improve on your work later when you come up with a new idea.

4. Most colleges offer free tutoring. The tutors will read over your paper or assignment and almost always give you valuable assistance that you would never have considered. Return to #3, to do this you must complete your assignment ahead of time.

5. Have a backup plan or two. Murphy's Law says: (1) Anything that can go wrong will, (2) Nothing is as easy as it looks, (3) Everything takes longer than you think it will.

6. Save your documents – often. The worst thing is when you lose a file, your computer turns off or malware attacks your files. Google Drive is fine for some things, but there are pitfalls.

7. Develop a solid notetaking system that works for you. You will need it for the rest of your life. Small things slip through the cracks. Checklists are extremely helpful.

8. There is never enough time. Bring enough clothes so you do not need to wash them as often. When you do wash them, take them out when they are done or else someone else will and you may never find them again.

9. Register for classes the minute the classes open up for you. Trust me on this one. Otherwise, you get a bad professor at a horrible time that conflicts with your commitments. You might not even get into prerequisites which extend your time in college.

10. Petition to get into a class. Begging is fine. The professor can say no, but at least you tried.

11. If you have any academic problem with illness, family, or an emergency, let your professors know immediately. Most will not care if you wait for a month thinking that you can handle it on your own.

12. Make a calendar and keep track of what you need to accomplish.

13. Teamwork is a mantra in college. You will work on teams. A few members are likely to be unmotivated slackers or talented, but extreme procrastinators. Determine this ahead of time and set intermediate goals. Remember, your grade is on the line. It's not fair but go back to #5. In the end, finish the project anyway. The unmotivated slacker will get an A, which may thoroughly make you frustrated, but you will too.

14. Book prices vary widely. The bookstore at the university is often not the cheapest. I have friends who swear by certain places where they always buy textbooks, get coupons, and then buy more books. However, the advantage of buying books in digital format is that you can often use 'Control F' to find the information you need and sometimes take digital notes, which is impossible with a physical copy. I prefer physical books, but you choose. Also, renting books is okay unless you forget to send the book back.

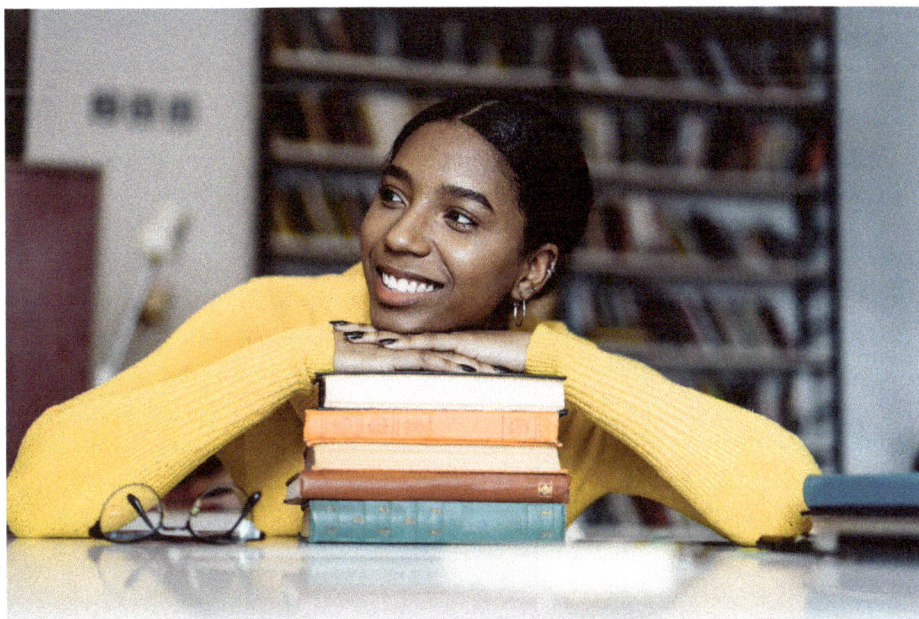

15. Get involved as soon as you can. Meet students who have similar interests. Join clubs, learn about the school's traditions, try activities you always wanted to learn, ask professors about volunteering on research projects, and get involved with intramural sports.

16. Don't bring a car. A car sounds wonderful, offering you freedom until your vehicle is broken into, the gas runs out, the car breaks down before a test, or you get a half dozen parking tickets. You never realized how much trouble a car could be on campus where there is limited and expensive parking.

17. Communicate with your professors. Most of them have office hours. Well, they probably all have office hours, but sometimes they are absent. Either drop by or make an appointment. Especially if you have a question or a problem, speak to them. A professor rarely helps a student after they turn in grades but may have excellent advice during the term if they are struggling. Surprisingly, also sometimes, the answer key is wrong. Occasionally, they are intimidating, standoffish, or mean-spirited. Fortunately, there are only a few bad ones, and even these professors teach you important lessons.

18. Don't get so excited about credit cards. Credit card companies will continually hound you to sign up with tempting offers. College students are prime targets because they do not yet really understand how challenging it is to pay them off monthly when there are so many things to purchase. You will probably have to learn the hard way, but they are not the savior they purport to be. Furthermore, you will likely spend more than you imagined, and the interest payments will dig you into a deep hole.

19. Drinking and drugs are around you 24/7. It does not matter what school you attend. Rarely is a campus void of alcohol or drugs. However, some colleges have more – much more. Some students will even sell illegal drugs in the dorm. You need to use your own judgment. Be careful. Students consume more than they realize, make judgment errors, get seriously injured, die of overdoses, and spread STDs. This piece was not written to scare you but to make you aware of the life-changing realities.

20. During Christmas break starting your first year, apply for internships, training opportunities, co-ops, or jobs for the summer. Create a resume. Getting experience cannot be understated if you want to jump on the job market and get real-world experience. Career fairs are extremely helpful so you can see what kind of job you might want. Every college has a career center. Get to know the people there.

21. Go boldly into this world and try new things. Thomas Edison once said, "I have not failed. I've just found 10,000 ways that won't work."

CHAPTER 8

FINANCIAL AID AND SCHOLARSHIPS: FINDING MONEY TO PAY FOR COLLEGE

"We are continually faced by great opportunities brilliantly disguised as insoluble problems."

– Lee Iacocca

FINANCIAL AID

R ISD, SVA, Cal Arts, NYU, and SAIC stand out for 3D art and design with amazing faculty, excellent facilities, and easy access to internships. While most students consider New York City for the top college art programs and internships, they should not discount other major metropolitan areas like Chicago and Los Angeles as well as cities around the country that are meccas for artists and journalists. However, you cannot go wrong going to RISD for its deep dive into the world of art. These colleges offer a rigorous course of study and socially responsible projects on the cutting edge of art, design, and forward-thinking optimism.

Nearly every university in the United States offers money for college. These funds come in the form of grants/scholarships that do not need to be paid back, loans that need to be repaid, and 'work study', where you are paid for a job associated with the college or university. Grants or scholarships are either need-based or merit-based. Need-based means that the college or government determines that, based on your income, you will be unable to attend without additional resources. Merit-based means that the college or university is offering you money based on some combination of your grades, test scores, skills, and/or talent.

For the 2022-2023 school year, the maximum Federal Pell Grant award for 2022-2023 is $6,895 and may be used at any university where the student is eligible. A new simplified FAFSA form opens in October 2023 for the 2024-2025 academic year.

To obtain need-based financial aid, almost all colleges require you to submit the Free Application for Federal Student Aid (FAFSA) found at www.studentaid.gov. Some colleges also require the College Scholarship Service (CSS) Profile which is available on the College Board website at www.collegeboard. org. Both the FAFSA and CSS Profile require your income based upon the tax returns you file with the U.S. federal government.

Most people will be able to download the tax information directly into the FAFSA form using the Data Retrieval Tool (DRT). This automatic process not only saves time, but the DRT also ensures that the correct information goes into the right locations on the form. Check anyway afterward since there could be an error. If your family has not filed a tax return yet, you can estimate the amounts. However, all income and other financial information will eventually need to be verified for you to receive need-based aid.

SCHOLARSHIPS

Harvard announced that beginning in the 2022-2023 students whose families make less than $75,000 will pay nothing for college. At Princeton University, families whose income is less than $65,000 will pay nothing as well. At UPenn, families with incomes less than $65,000 per year not only do not pay for tuition, room, and board, but they are eligible for laptop funds and summer opportunity support. To recap, the Ivy League colleges have put college affordability first with free tuition for students from low-income families. Lookup any of these schools and you will be surprised at how little college costs for an Ivy League education.

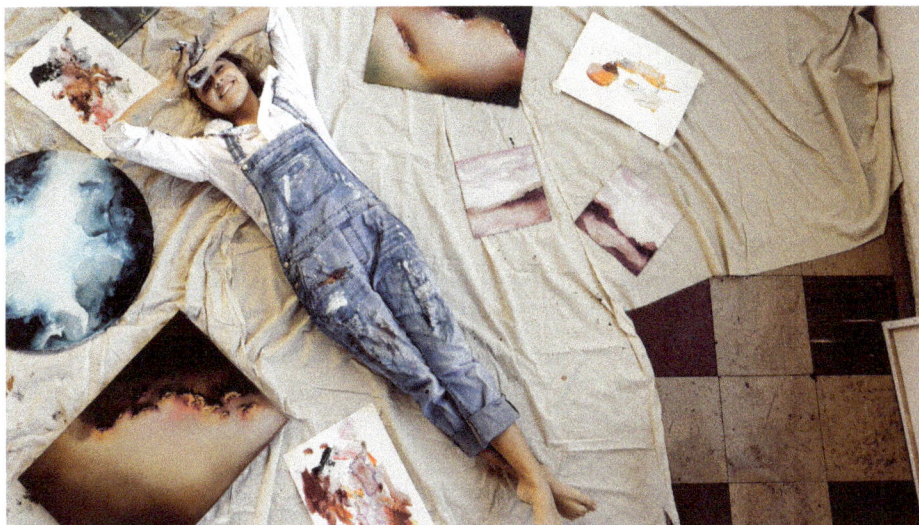

Most colleges offer merit aid, though some of the top colleges in the country like Stanford, MIT, Caltech, and the Ivy League do not offer scholarship money based on academics or talent. Thus, the cost for private colleges vary widely based on how generous they are with need-based and merit-based money.

Merit scholarships offered through a college or university that are based upon academic success may have additional forms and essays to complete. Merit scholarships based upon talent typically require a portfolio, performance, audition, or some other demonstration of skills. Also, check the specific art, dance, music, writing, theatre, research, robotics, engineering, or program to see what the college requires. Note: Each college or university has a different set of rules for what and how you submit your art, video, writing samples, or other demonstration of your mastery.

Please check out the profile section at the back of this book for scholarships and requirements. Additionally, look up the college website for their financial aid process. To help you get a sense of available scholarships, I selected six schools at random from the options listed in the profile section.

ArtCenter College of Design

ArtCenter offers more than $22 million in scholarships for students with need and talent each year. Amounts vary based on need, talent, available funds, and recommendations from the scholarship committee. ArtCenter offers continuing scholarships for students currently in school.

Columbia College Chicago

Columbia College offers merit and need-based scholarships to more than a hundred freshmen, transfer, and graduate students. Most of the scholarships are renewable each year with given GPA and coursework requirements. Columbia College meets four years of full-need of both domestic and international applicants. For merit scholarships, creative samples must be submitted with the application. Full tuition awards are also available.

Pratt Institute

Pratt offers generous merit-based scholarships. Sixty percent of incoming first-year students are offered merit-based awards for their talent. In addition, Pratt has restricted and endowed scholarships along with its need-based financial aid program. International students are also eligible for merit-based awards. No additional application is required for prospective students; all admitted students are considered automatically.

Rhode Island School of Design

RISD offers scholarships to students who demonstrate academic and talent-based success and financial need. Many students receive $20,000 awards. However, scholarships are need-based, and international students must pay the full tuition.

Savannah College of Art and Design (SCAD)

Some colleges are exceptionally generous with money for a large proportion of students. For example, at SCAD, 80% of new applicants receive merit & need-based scholarships. These opportunities are available for U.S. citizens, permanent residents, and international students.

Syracuse University

Syracuse University students received more than $400 million in financial aid. Syracuse offers internal merit-based scholarships and supports students in finding external funds as well. Merit-based funding is offered to more than 35% of the incoming class. Approximately 80% of SU's incoming students received some type of financial support. Syracuse University offers a financial aid package to incoming students that meet full-need.

PRIVATE SCHOLARSHIPS

Some scholarship money available does not come directly from the college. Private individuals, corporations, and endowments offer outside scholarships for students who apply. Some of these scholarships are significant. A few offer full tuition. Here are a few of the thousands to consider.

Gates Millennium Scholarship

Full scholarships are granted to 300 ethnic minority students per year to attend any U.S. college or university.

Questbridge Scholarship

$200,000 is granted to each of 1,464 students to be used over 4 years.

Hispanic Scholarship Fund

Approximately 10,000 winners - $30,000,000 awarded annually.

Thurgood Marshall College Fund

African Americans – approximately 500 scholarships per year (average award - $6,200 per year).

NAACP – National Association for the Advancement of Colored People

African Americans - about 170 students receive awards of $3,000 to $15,000.

Coca Cola Scholarship

1,400 students win scholarships (total amount awarded annually is approximately $3,550,000).

150 students receive $20,000 scholarship each.

NASSP – National Association of Secondary School Principals

600 NHS Scholarships awarded per year, 1 national winner ($25,000 scholarship).

24 national finalists ($5,625 each), 575 national semifinalists ($3,200 each).

Apply between October 1 and December 1.

GE-Reagan Foundation Scholarship Program

$40,000 (10 students)

Another $50,000 is awarded in the Great Communicator Debate Series.

Scholastic Art and Writing Competition

Herblock Award - $1,000 scholarships for editorial cartoons

New York Life Award - $1,000 writing award about personal grief and loss

One Earth Award - $1,000 scholarship for writing about human-caused climate change

Portfolio Scholarships – Up to $10,000 granted for top portfolios

Civic Expression Award - $1,000 scholarships for writing on political and social issues

Best-In-Grade – Juror favorite awards receive $500 scholarships

College Tuition & Summer Scholarships - https://www.artandwriting.org/scholarships/

Gloria Barron Prize for Young Heroes

25 students each year ages 8 – 18 receive $10,000 for community service projects.

Prudential Spirit of Community Award (Prudential Emerging Visionaries)

25 students in grades 5 to 12 are granted a $1,000 - $5,000 award for community service.

Comcast NBCUniversal Leaders and Achievers Scholarship

More than 800 high school student winners each year win a $2,500 scholarship.

Brower Youth Awards

Environmental activism awards are granted to 6 winners; each receives $3,000.

Target Scholarship

HBCU Design Challenge for African Americans – Students submit designs for Black History Month.

Target Scholars Program – 1,000 students get $5,000 each.

New Tang Dynasty Television International Figure Painting Competition 2023

Submit a high-resolution photograph of artwork, resume, application

Gold Award - $10,000; Silver Award - $3,000; Bronze Award - $1,500

Outstanding Technique - $1,000 each; Profound Humanities Award - $1,000 each

Outstanding Youth Award - $1,000 each; Honorable Mention Awards

Service/Leadership/Focused Organization Scholarship

Lions Club, Moose Club, Elks Club, Rotary Club, Soroptimists Club, Mensa

Parent Employment

Many companies offer scholarships for their employees and their children.

K-12 Educator Scholarship

This scholarship is for children with parents who teach in the K-12 system.

Distinguished Scholars Awards, Art Contest Scholarships

There are numerous scholarships that fall into these categories.

ROTC

These military scholarships are not given to everyone in ROTC.

A select group of outstanding candidates is given tuition, fees, textbooks, plus a monthly stipend.

CHAPTER 9

SUPPLEMENTAL MATERIALS AND PORTFOLIOS FOR 3D ART & DESIGN PROGRAMS

"When you are content to be simply yourself and don't compare or compete, everyone will respect you."

– Lao Tzu

S urprise colleges with your art. Demonstrate your curiosity, intelligence, and innovative thinking. Colleges want to see what they have never seen. Admissions representatives want to be amazed. What are your muses? What are your passions? What do you find meaningful? What social, political, or experiential ideas frame your art? What sets you apart?

Students pursuing 3D art and design are encouraged to keep sketchbooks on the road to art school. These show growth, ideas, muses, and skill. Bring these to a portfolio review. The drawings you compile say quite a bit about you and your interests.

At the top art and design schools like Rhode Island School of Design, School of Visual Arts, New York University, CalArts, Parsons School of Design, School of the Art Institute of Chicago, and Washington University in St. Louis, acceptance is very difficult. Furthermore, the BFA degree is completely immersive. Inspired by the environment, you will be surrounded by students who are creative, multitalented, and focused.

Students must be wholly dedicated to art. Thus, admissions officers and art school directors are keenly interested in the applicant's talent and commitment. As a result, a portfolio review is required for the top schools; sometimes, an interview is part of the admissions process as well. Applicants must demonstrate ability and potential.

CHANGES IN THE APPLICANT DEMOGRAPHICS
CHALLENGES ON THE ROAD AHEAD

COVID-19 shook students as well as admissions offices. Many studio-centered programs closed down or went online. International students left for their country of origin and classes at a distance could not provide the needed materials, space, and opportunities. Many quit and did not return.

Furthermore, some art programs completely shut down. Colleges faced a crisis. While some programs reopened after COVID-19 and some students returned, demographic shifts resulted, including gender diversity and ethnic makeup. Additionally, the decreased population of international students altered art programs. Nevertheless, many students still applied.

Other challenges existed as well. COVID-19 changed the makeup of applicants to college. Many students of color chose not to apply. Other data show that while enrollments rebounded, some programs suffered from budget cuts.

NATIONAL PORTFOLIO DAYS

These online and in-person national events are free for students to participate anywhere they are located in the world. In-person events are often held both inside and outside of the United States. Prospective art program applicants have the chance to meet admissions staff and present art pieces. Students must register online. There are filters with the online registration so you can sign up for events that fit your needs: online in-person, undergraduates, transfer, or graduate school.

In-person events can be jam-packed with people, though COVID-19 changed procedures with limited numbers of individuals inside venues. In the past, massive lines accumulated as students waited their turn. Latecomers were often very disappointed, surprised by seeing the huge crowds. In some locations, now, there is a reservation system. Make sure you read about any required protocols for in-person events.

More than fifty colleges come to many of the in-person events. Typically, you will have 10 to 15 minutes to speak to a representative and show them your work. You should bring a range of pieces. The website recommends bringing 10 – 12 pieces. Even if you only bring five, you are fine. The point is for your work to be reviewed so you can gain valuable feedback and improve.

For the online events, there are live sessions where you wait in a 'waiting room' queue until you can be seen. You can also schedule a meeting, though only on the day of the event. You may register for multiple school reviews. Note that you will not upload your portfolio. Rather, you will meet with your reviewer via Zoom and share your screen.

These events do not guarantee admission, and no admissions decisions are made at these events. In addition, although the colleges may suggest that you apply for their scholarships or be considered for their merit awards, you will not be awarded any money at these events.

In most cases, you will still need to present your portfolio online through the school-determined application portal. Even so, these events are excellent in that they allow you to meet people from various colleges and they get a chance to meet you. Furthermore, you get helpful advice and suggestions on how you can improve the pieces you plan to submit.

ART SCHOOL ADMISSIONS

RISD offers its own portfolio days online, where they will review your work and give you a valuable critique. Hint: RISD looks for engaged learners who will connect with the world. They want art that says something meaningful, evokes emotion and shares a point of view. Being technically strong is essential, but being emotionally strong and inextricably linked to the audience is imperative. Thus, more is not better. Only share your best work.

Portfolios are required at many art colleges. Since students often apply to 10-20 schools, the effort can be daunting. Furthermore, completing applications and creating portfolios take time and money for training, preparation, application fees, and other expenses. For some schools, there are fee waivers.

PORTFOLIO REQUIREMENTS

The first entry point to art programs is investigating colleges. Apply to your dream school, but also select colleges that have programs that fit your criteria – classes, program requirements, geography, studio space, faculty, career prospects, cost, etc. For now, let's look at the portfolio requirements at a few schools. Start by getting a general idea of what each school requires so that you are prepared. More information is provided in the profiles later on in this book.

CALIFORNIA INSTITUTE OF THE ARTS

4-year BFA in Art

Students must complete the online application, fees, artist statement, two letters of recommendation, and transcripts. In the CalArts portfolio section, include 15-20 images of any medium. A variety of types of work is preferred. Sketches or works in progress are acceptable. Do not use a pre-formatted portfolio as images must be individual, not composited, PDFs, or website links. Make sure the image fills the slide. Provide captions, descriptions, and titles in the "edit details" area. Do not include generic work like technical exercises, figure/life drawings, or still life drawings. You will also submit a 30-90 second video introduction.

NEW YORK UNIVERSITY

BFA Studio Art

After completing the Common Application, students will submit an "Artistic Review" from your application status page. Media uploads can include images of artwork (drawing, painting, sculpture, video, photography, digital art, etc.) that represents your artistic interests while also demonstrating your technical abilities and imagination. You must include 12-15 images of recent artwork in any medium. You will also present a one-page "Statement of Purpose".

PARSONS SCHOOL OF ART AND DESIGN

BFA Fine Arts; BFA Communication Design

Parsons requests an uploaded portfolio of eight to twelve images from a student's breadth of media skills, including drawing, painting, sculpture, design, collage, animation, etc. Experimentation, imagination, and self-expression are key. Include documentation and descriptions of your work and process. Parsons also requires a submission called "The Parsons Challenge". Start this part early. Many students put this off, and either do a lackluster job or cannot pull this together before the deadline. The Parsons Challenge is a new visual work inspired by a theme expressed in work within the portfolio. Students submit a required 500-word essay describing the development of the idea. Two additional pieces may be added to document your process. Observational work is not required since technique and vision are emphasized in the review.

RHODE ISLAND SCHOOL OF DESIGN

BFA Painting
Concentration Option in Drawing

After completing the Common Application, students will submit a SlideRoom supplement. Students present 12-20 of their recent work on the SlideRoom site. RISD requests finished pieces, drawings from direct observation, and no more than three pieces that show research and prep work. RISD's admissions are competitive, so you should curate and edit the pieces you choose to submit in your portfolio.

SCHOOL OF THE ART INSTITUTE OF CHICAGO

BFA Painting & Drawing
BFA Art & Technology Studies
BFA Visual Communication Design

Submit the Common Application, noting the merit scholarship deadlines and specific requirements. All programs require a SlideRoom portfolio. Develop the 250-500-word artist's statement describing how and why you created the pieces you submitted and how your experiences contributed to your thinking. Include 10-15 creative works that demonstrate your potential from observational to abstract. All media are considered, though SAIC suggests submitting those that are bold, inventive, thought-provoking, expressive, and risk-taking. You may concentrate on a single media or any combination of include drawings, prints, photographs, paintings, film, video, audio recordings, sculpture, ceramics, fashion designs, graphic design, furniture, objects, architectural designs, websites, video games, sketchbooks, scripts, storyboards, screenplays, and zines.

SCHOOL OF VISUAL ARTS

BFA Fine Arts
Concentrations: Painting, Drawing, Printmaking, Sculpture, & Installation

Apply through the SVA site and submit a portfolio of 15-20 images of your strongest artwork through SlideRoom. Include samples of your drawing with a minimum of 3-5 examples from direct observation (self-portraits, figure drawings, object studies, still life, and landscape). Other media, like painting, photography, printmaking, collage, etc., are welcome. Sketchbooks, shown at in-person reviews, offer valuable insights. Do not focus on computer-generated images.

WASHINGTON UNIVERSITY IN ST. LOUIS

BFA Art
Concentrations in Painting, Photography, Printmaking,
Sculpture, Time-Based + Media Art
BA Art; BA Design

After completing the Common Application, College of Art students will submit a SlideRoom supplement. All art applicants are considered for the Conway or Poretz Scholarship in art. Media uploads of 12 – 15 images can include recent work drawings, 2D pieces, 3D models, photography, video, etc.

CHAPTER 10

POST PANDEMIC EMPLOYMENT OUTLOOK: STATISTICS AND ECONOMIC PROJECTIONS

"In every walk with nature one receives far more than he seeks."

– John Muir

Artists often enter many different fields and play essential roles in society. According to the *Occupational Outlook Handbook*, employment opportunities in these fields are slated to grow from 2020 to 2030 at different rates with new jobs expected. The median annual wage for entry-level positions is given below. The job outlook for artists is good with a 14% growth rate. Wages are also likely to increase.

According to the 2022 Bureau of Labor Statistics,[1]

OCCUPATION	JOB SUMMARY	ENTRY-LEVEL EDUCATION	MEDIAN PAY
Advertising Sales and Agents	Advertising sales agents sell advertising space to businesses and individuals.	High School Diploma or Equivalent	$54,940
Archivists, Curators, and Museum Workers	Archivists and curators oversee institutions' collections, such as historical items or of artwork. Museum technicians and conservators prepare and restore items in those collections.	Varies	$52,140
Art Directors	Art directors are responsible for the visual style and images in magazines, newspapers, product packaging, and movie and television productions.	Bachelor's Degree	$97,270
Broadcast, Sound, and Video Technicians	Broadcast, sound, and video technicians set up, operate, and maintain the electrical equipment for media programs.	Varies	$50,000
Craft and Fine Artists	Craft and fine artists use a variety of materials and techniques to create art for sale and exhibition.	Varies	$49,120
Dancers and Choreographers	Dancers and choreographers use dance performances to express ideas and stories.	Varies	N/A/
Desktop Publishers	Desktop publishers use computer software to design page layouts for items that are printed or published online.	Associate's Degree	$47,560
Editors	Editors plan, review, and revise content for publication.	Bachelor's Degree	$63,400
OCCUPATION	**JOB SUMMARY**	**ENTRY-LEVEL EDUCATION**	**MEDIAN PAY**
Fashion Designers	Fashion designers create clothing, accessories, and footwear.	Bachelor's Degree	$75,810

OCCUPATION	JOB SUMMARY	ENTRY-LEVEL EDUCATION	MEDIAN PAY
Film and Video Editors & Camera Operators	Film and video editors and camera operators manipulate moving images that entertain or inform an audience.	Bachelor's Degree	$61,900
Graphic Designers	Graphic designers create visual concepts, using computer software or by hand, to communicate ideas that inspire, inform, and captivate consumers.	Bachelor's Degree	$53,380
Industrial Designers	Industrial designers combine art, business, and engineering to develop the concepts for manufactured products.	Bachelor's Degree	$71,640
Jewelers & Precious Stone & Metal Workers	Jewelers and precious stone and metal workers design, construct, adjust, repair, appraise and sell jewelry.	Bachelor's Degree	$41,900
Market Research Analysts	Market research analysts study market conditions to examine potential sales of a product or service.	Bachelor's Degree	$65,810
News Analysts, Reporters, and Journalists	News analysts, reporters, and journalists keep the public updated about current events and noteworthy information.	Bachelor's Degree	$49,300
Public Relations & Fundraising Managers	Public relations managers direct the creation of materials that will enhance the public image of their employer or client. Fundraising managers coordinate campaigns that bring in donations for their organization.	Bachelor's Degree	$118,430
Public Relations Specialists	Public relations specialists create and maintain a positive public image for the clients they represent.	Bachelor's Degree	$62,810
Sales Managers	Sales managers direct organizations' sales teams.	Bachelor's Degree	$132,290
Photographers	Photographers use their technical expertise, creativity, and composition skills to produce and preserve images.	Bachelor's Degree	$41,280

OCCUPATION	JOB SUMMARY	ENTRY-LEVEL EDUCATION	MEDIAN PAY
Special Effects Artists & Animators	Special effects artists and animators create images that appear to move and visual effects for various forms of media and entertainment.	Bachelor's Degree	$77,700
Technical Writers	Technical writers prepare instruction manuals, how-to guides, journal articles, and other supporting documents to communicate complex and technical information more easily.	Bachelor's Degree	$74,650
Woodworkers	Woodworkers manufacture a variety of products, such as cabinets and furniture, using wood, veneers, and laminates.	High School Diploma or Equivalent	$33,750
Writers and Authors	Writers and authors develop written content for various types of media.	Bachelor's Degree	$67,120

We know what we are but know not what we may be.

– William Shakespeare

Artists work in studios where they immortalize ideas in a job that is a cross between artist, Imagineer, and digital content expert. The median pay for an artist is $49,120 for those with a bachelor's degree. Those with a master's degree are typically paid higher due to their more specialized, focused knowledge. The employment prospects for artists are positive with 7,000 new jobs expected in 2022.

Similar jobs, listed in the previous chart, vary across subjects since artists have different focuses. The fluidity and opportunity in art across travel, nature, marketing, journalism, and fashion run the gamut of options, not to mention scuplture work. Society has a wide and varied use for the skills of an artist. However, you will need to discover your personal areas of interest.

The skills an art student learns in school, including drawing, painting, graphic design, printmaking, package design, illustration, comic book art, collage, sculpture, ceramics, crafts, and computer-aided design are valuable and transferrable to other fields as well. According to the Bureau of Labor Statistics, approximately 54% of artists are self-employed while 7% work in the federal government, 7% in independent jobs, 5% in the motion picture and sound recording industries, and 3% work in personal care services. The remaining hold various other positions.[2]

IMPACT OF COVID-19

COVID-19 impacted the number of jobs people could get in art. A significant drop in opportunities led most artists to the internet to post their art and set up their independent work for freelancing. The dynamic changed as Pinterest, Instagram, and Facebook became inundated with images. One of my friends in the publishing business said that freelancers needed a "megaphone" or "gimmick" to get noticed. He is not a gimmicky kind of guy, so he searches for platforms to broadcast his work. Thus, the impact of COVID-19 cannot be understated. While artistic fields are booming with more entrants presenting what they create, practicing continues to be essential, and technique can always be improved.

ROAD TO BECOMING AN ARTIST

The road to success in this industry should not be discouraging since a few steps are required along the way. Even so, achieving the goal is rewarding. Encourage those around you. If this is the field you want to pursue, pave the road in front of you and drive.

One or two internships or apprenticeships in peripheral areas would not hurt you in your pursuit of gigs and contract work. Although some internships are

---

2   Bureau of Labor Statistics, U.S. Department of Labor, *Occupational Outlook Handbook*, Craft and Fine Artists, at https://www.bls.gov/ooh/arts-and-design/craft-and-fine-artists.htm

unpaid, you will find that most applicants will have one or more. Some internships pay fairly well. Even if you ultimately be a freelancer, you might find parallel professions that put food on the table while you fine-tune your craft.

If you are serious, you will make a fantastic career out of your pursuit. Initiative-taking persistence, talent, creativity, and moxie can get you into your desired college program and career. You may have to start at the very bottom of the ladder, but you can climb the rungs methodically one by one.

Companies want to know employees' work ethic, personality, and professionalism. An internship allows you to get to know the corporate climate better and allows others to get to know you better too. Thus, many companies hire the interns they feel are the best fit rather than choosing candidates from the piles of resumes that have been submitted.

Education unlocks doors no matter which direction your career takes you. Whatever direction you pursue, if you lay a foundation, undaunted by the competition, and are unafraid of starting at the bottom, you will do fine. Hard work and creativity go a long way in this industry. Start by getting a solid education.

MANAGEMENT AND EMPLOYEE RETENTION

Skills to Know: Management, Human Resources, Social Consciousness, Ethics

One of the most significant challenges facing employers in the years from 2022 - 2030 will be locating and retaining talent. The pandemic slowed education

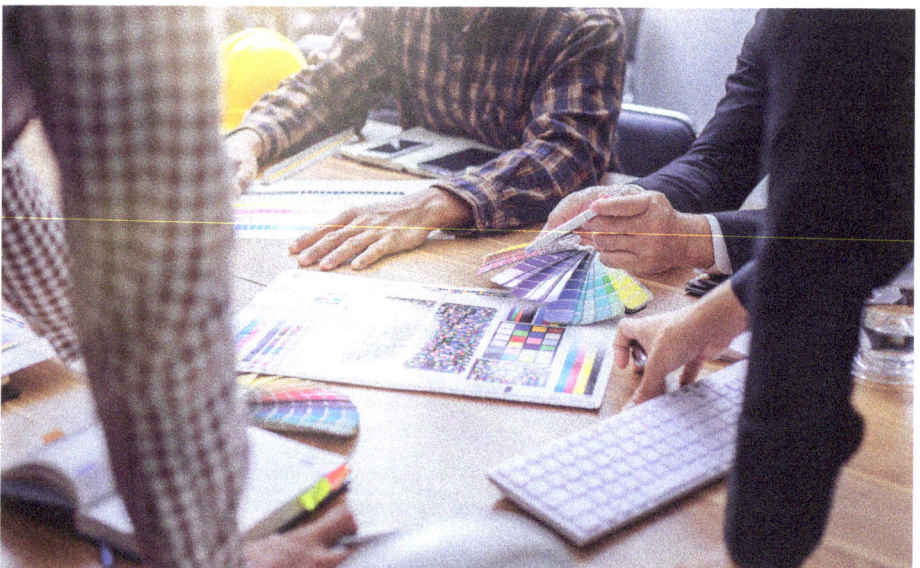

and learning with online classes, reduced access to faculty/advising, limited access to labs, inability to attend workshops, retail closures, and fewer conferences, meetings, and shows. Health concerns rose to the top of importance as did financial stress, job uncertainty, and social consciousness.

Many students chose to work rather than study and start online stores when they could not access locations for community service or continue with their sport, instrument, or hobbies. With the changes in lifestyle and fears about health, safety, and wellness, many bright and talented students developed a fearless sense of autonomy and independence, while for others, the necessary skills ordinarily developed in school were fraught by limitations.

Finding talent within the changing hiring atmosphere will require new skills to retain staff. Employees are increasingly looking elsewhere for a better opportunity. This development will require managers to earn and harness employee trust and loyalty.

The digital workforce has also placed demands on human resources. While many companies want their employees to work in-person, the convenience of working at home and the drudgery of commuting to work have created an environment where employees seek greater flexibility. Changes are coming. The employee talent challenge is likely to create a more global workforce where companies look for less expensive online talent from a pool of eager workers in other countries.

CHAPTER 11

NEXT STEPS: PREPARATION AND REAL-WORLD SKILLS

"The one who plants trees, knowing that he will never sit in their shade, has at least started to understand the meaning of life."

– Rabindranath Tagore

Collage offers you the freedom to express yourself openly, dynamically, and interactively. As you explore art in society, you will explore the art within you, hungering to emerge. The next step for you is to choose a college where your persona fits into the makeup of the environment. In college studios, you will receive personalized, interactive training, immersed and infused with inspiration from fellow classmates.

Each drawing or painting you produce will leave a lasting impression. Through social media, instantaneously, you can share your art with millions of people in a matter of moments. The possibilities are limitless. In school or out of school, you may want to take a few classes on social media dynamics and website editing. Furthermore, on the leading edge of the Metaverse, you can create opportunities that were never before possible. It's unbelievably thrilling.

Art is a dynamic, multidimensional world where you contribute to the dialogue. In some careers, repetitive tasks and uninspiring projects lead employees to loathe their jobs and tick off minutes until their day is done. Yet, your life will undoubtedly be different and ever-changing since the world around you will change from moment to moment. Over time, whichever area of art becomes your focus, you will earn your way to a career of endless possibilities.

American landscape painter, George Inness, shared, "The true use of art is, first, to cultivate the artist's own spiritual nature." Spend time thinking, even though time sometimes seems short. You may feel as if time slips through your fingers like sand in an hourglass. Resist the temptation to upload your art before contemplating what you want to express. While social media opens doors to share your artwork, truly magical works are created when time stands still, and you immerse yourself in a creative state.

Today is a precious moment. As you contemplate college choices and tomorrow's future, you will explore your passion, open doors you never expected, and discover opportunities that will tantalize and challenge you along the way. As such, you will capture a new, exciting, and eclectic way of life.

Attending a respected school can help you get noticed. Your next steps are aided by connections offered by professors, classmates, and alumni. Networking at events is also an excellent way to discover opportunities. Shows, displays, and contests in school, out of school, in the summer, or through social media can help you get noticed. Bring people into your world, allowing them to feel and interpret art in their unique way.

Throughout your varied experiences, you will meet other artists who may recommend you or inform you about open positions or contract opportunities, even some that are not publicly announced. In addition, many schools have a culminating event where you can put your best foot forward and showcase your work. Exposure to industry professionals can open new doors while interacting with people online or in-person will allow you to maintain those connections.

Autonomy and freedom to choose the jobs you take by venturing out on your own may seem alluring, but freelancing may result in uncertainty or even career limitations. As a result, companies often choose seasoned professionals with work experience in other firms. However, there are ways to mitigate against the lean times of solo work. A few options include demonstrating mastery, producing amazing work, resolving client problems, aligning ideologies, and initially charging less. Despite challenges, put yourself out there.

You could wait for the phone to ring to be discovered. However, you should post regularly and be out and about for that to happen. Some individuals pine away, hoping to be selected and deciding which organization would be a perfect fit. Others decide that they only want to work at a specific firm or location. Still others determine that they will work for themselves and be their own boss. Yet, sometimes taking any position at the start is a steppingstone to your dream life, commitment to service, and opportunity to put your unique mark on society.

BOLD NETWORKING

Networking takes social skills and a bit of moxie. From elevator speeches and professional encounters to interviews and masterclasses, your job is to find a way to get your work in front of people and have them see your talent and your potential to contribute. You have something special and fresh ideas. Finally, there is a professional entity that will welcome your style, ingenuity, discipline, and impact.

How can you be recognized? Meet people; hand out your resume; give them your business card; ask for their business card; follow up; ask if you can call or meet them, even when approaching these professionals may seem uncomfortable. Stay in touch with people you meet, even if it is just happenstance or serendipity. Keep a log with each person's phone, e-mail, identifying information, and both date and location where you met. You never know when you will need it.

If you meet people professionally at a masterclass or workshop, even if you do not exchange information, you will recognize them at a later date. They may recognize you in a future event too. Keep training. You should always seek ways to improve, irrespective of your experience. Lifelong learning improves your ability to maintain up-to-date skills and transition to new ventures. The outside world's perspective changes more quickly with social media's instant influences.

Though you should not take workshops just for the sake of meeting people, when you attend, be present in your quest to lead, serve, and envision. If your focus is not on your improvement or development, you may appear insincere in your intentions. However, workshops, conferences, and contests can allow others to see your purpose, vision, and talent.

Big-ticket training does not always mean better trainers or opportunities. Find time to visit museums, survey your surroundings, and notice cultural changes. While gathering new thoughts, remember humility and open-mindedness go a long way. Defer to the wise and listen. There is much you can learn.

STAY IN TOUCH

Do not annoy busy people, but you can keep in touch every couple of months. Communicating more frequently is overwhelming. However, life is long. People who grow with their craft transition fluidly through life's career phases. In drawing and painting, contacts are essential in all phases of your career. Also, do not be surprised. Many go-getters seeking to gain a coveted contract do the following:

1. Speak at Chamber of Commerce meetings.
2. Attend art, design, and software trade shows.
3. Gain a following on Instagram and Pinterest.
4. Write a newsletter and publish it on LinkedIn and other sources.
5. Link your work to Facebook, Twitter, Instagram, Pinterest, and other social media.
6. Enter in art contests.
7. Join professional associations.
8. Attend social gatherings of potential customers.
9. Keep in touch with your professors.
10. Stay involved with your alumni associations.

Friendships matter. Become lifelong colleagues by finding friends who share mutual interests and offer a sounding board or connections to new opportunities. People tend to stay in touch with "important" people. Note to self: Your contemporaries or peers are important people...although possibly not yet. As you form lists of contacts, you are likely to know these people throughout your career.

Be audacious while also being authentic. Networking can sometimes appear fake or forced as if you are going out on a hunt to find people for your own benefit. Worse, the act of networking can appear like stalking for those who incessantly attempt to connect.

The mental image of this type of 'networking' conjures the vision of people congregating at meetings. Friendships and the mutual support of allies can be enormously helpful, though 20,000 or even 200,000 followers on your website do not mean you are popular. However, you can have unexpected meaningful exchanges if you get out, meet people, and live life.

There are times when deeply moving, casual conversations in non-professional settings could also turn into connections. Do not lose touch with people or burn bridges along the way. This industry is not that big, especially in the subspecialty you choose. You will continually see extraordinary talent. You never know. They may contact you to collaborate one day or meet for coffee at an event.

COLLEGE AND CAREER CENTERS

Although art programs often have internal connections to help you secure an internship or job, you might also speak to someone at your campus career center. They often have interesting and possibly different prospects you might not get elsewhere. In addition, there may be a specific career liaison for their art programs. Connect with them for help in your search process. Besides, you might want a related job that utilizes your creative, design, problem-solving, and presentation skills.

Companies that attend art and design shows often hire graduates whose energy, initiative, and cutting-edge knowledge are invaluable. Design, camera, and software companies also appreciate those who can demonstrate their products. Adobe, for example, has more than 24,000 employees worldwide. These jobs may or may not be your dream job now, but you might be surprised where the position may lead you, and sometimes you just need employment to earn money and get yourself on your feet.

Career center coordinators often have excellent ideas of alternative options you may have never considered. Furthermore, they can assist you with creating a professional resume and cover letters for specific industries that are different from the ones you have for 3D art and design.

They may also connect you with past graduates in the industry who make excellent connections. Some of them may have been in your program and have been through the ropes, know a few people, and may be able to get you an interview or invite you to an industry event. Any contact may help you get your foot in the door or find a job to make money in the meantime.

LINKEDIN

LinkedIn is especially helpful for career searches. You can find numerous influential contacts on LinkedIn. After interviews or events, connect with each person you met on LinkedIn. Keep a contact list of individuals you get to know in your area of interest. Do not constantly try to connect with people you do not really know. However, if you have made the connection, occasionally keep in touch.

While some LinkedIn message boxes may be full and you may not get a reply, you can try. Some people have tens of thousands of LinkedIn followers. I have about 20,000 'contacts', which does not necessitate that I am important. Remember that a paycheck or lots of friends does not make you more worthy or successful. Worth and value emanate from within your heart. Occasionally, you hit on a lucky break. Though I do not have time to communicate with everyone, I have connected with some of my most inspiring authors, advisors, and intellectual leaders through LinkedIn.

FINALLY

Most people are willing to help you. Five percent will not. Thus, you have a 19 out of 20 chance of interacting with decent people who have the time and will give you advice. Don't lose faith in humanity just because you run into a few people who are too busy to stop for you or are too self-absorbed that they cannot answer your question.

Remember that talent is only the beginning. You need to sell yourself. As you organize your goals and responsibilities, remember to think one step ahead of where you want to be by making a game plan. Since actions speak louder than words, take action without complaining and spread kindness along the way. Burned bridges are tough to reconstruct.

Honesty and trustworthiness are worth more than any physical object. Earn this by working hard, being efficient, and telling the truth. Professionalism in your words and deeds is essential. Put away all distractions and focus on your tasks. Texts and social media take a surprising amount of time. Every action you take is a steppingstone to your future. Discipline is achieved by creating a goal and making it happen.

A nice note, card, or gift reminds people you are thinking about them, even when you are incredibly busy. Good friends who have your best interest may know doors that are not yet open for you. Keep in touch with them.

So, go on a walk, meet people, and live fully. Serendipity happens when you live life. However, your education is immensely valuable. Success happens when preparation meets opportunity. Thus, preparation is the best way to generate luck. Finally, even the most disciplined person can be lazy or inefficient. Fight this. Stay active. Make your life happen for you. Here are a few things to remember as you go out to pursue your dreams.

- Work ethic is everything.
- Excellence is expected.
- Learn what you do not know on your own time.
- Come to work prepared.
- Take constructive criticism well.
- Be respectful and courteous.
- Keep your cool under pressure.
- Avoid being timid.
- Stay on task.
- Come early.
- Stay late.
- Take your work seriously.
- Do more than expected.
- Be thoughtful and respectful.
- Read your e-mail/texts after hours in case something is important.
- Ask questions. No question is too stupid.
- Maintain a clean workspace.
- Dress and act professionally.
- Don't gossip or complain.
- Play when you are done.
- Avoid frustrating your phenomenally busy supervisor.
- Be straightforward, and don't beat around the bush.

You've Got This!

4
Regions

43
Programs

COLLEGE PROFILES AND REQUIREMENTS

WEST

MIDWEST

NORTHEAST

SOUTH

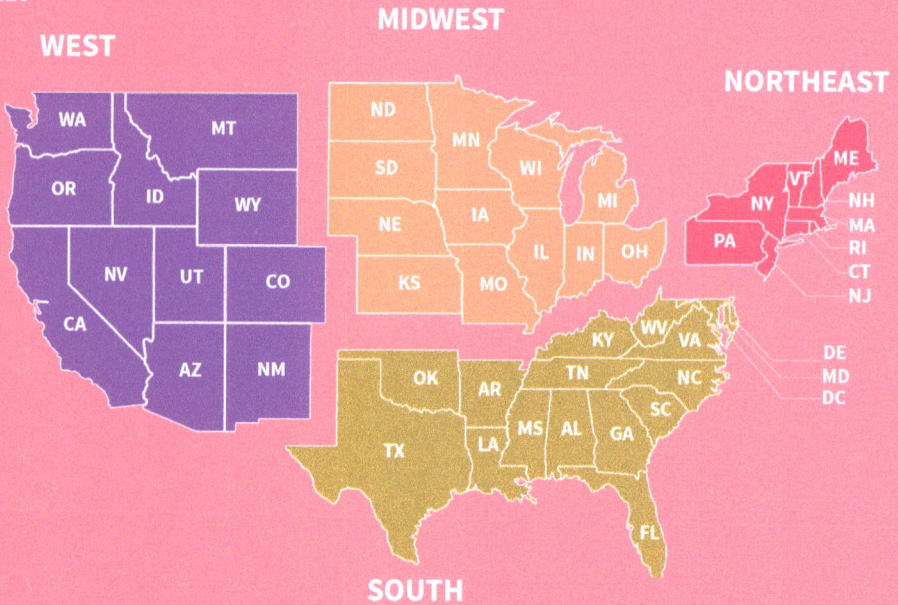

PROGRAMS BY REGION
U.S. CENSUS BUREAU CLASSIFICATIONS

REGION 1 – NORTHEAST

Connecticut, Maine, Massachusetts, New Hampshire, New Jersey, New York, Pennsylvania, Rhode Island, and Vermont

REGION 2 – MIDWEST

Illinois, Indiana, Iowa, Kansas, Michigan, Minnesota, Missouri, Nebraska, North Dakota, Ohio, South Dakota, and Wisconsin

REGION 3 – SOUTH

Alabama, Arkansas, Delaware, District of Columbia, Florida, Georgia, Kentucky, Louisiana, Maryland, Mississippi, North Carolina, Oklahoma, South Carolina, Tennessee, Texas, Virginia, and West Virginia

REGION 4 – WEST

Alaska, Arizona, California, Colorado, Hawaii, Idaho, Montana, Nevada, New Mexico, Oregon, Utah, Washington, and Wyoming

LIST OF SCULPTURE, CERAMICS, GLASS, & JEWELRY PROGRAMS

The 43 programs listed in the following pages include profiles of the top undergraduate art programs with a focus on sculpture, ceramics, glass, and jewelry design as of April 2022 along with a few additional college programs that offer closely related degrees like metalsmithing. Many students interested in 3D design are often also interested in drawing, painting, graphic art, industrial/product design, animation, and film. Those schools are profiled in other books, though some lists are provided in the back.

Majoring in 3D design is not for everyone. Although immensely rewarding, success requires initiative. Some students dual major for greater flexibility. In college, students discover their priorities, commitments, and perseverance. A few choose an alternative path somewhere down the road.

Thus, this book provides you with lists of additional art programs so you can explore those options. Keep the book handy. Even after you begin college, you may find that the summer and alternative college programs are helpful.

Creating lists is often tedious and cumbersome. These lists were gathered to help you with this task.

Descriptions of the college programs, tuition, requirements, and deadlines are accurate as of April 2022. However, the requirements may have changed by the time you purchase this book. Nevertheless, this information is a great place to start!

Note: To simplify the text and fit information into the charts and descriptions, abbreviations were used as well as shortened sentences and acronyms.

CONNECTICUT

MAINE

MASSACHUSETTS

NEW HAMPSHIRE

NEW JERSEY

NEW YORK

PENNSYLVANIA

RHODE ISLAND

VERMONT

CHAPTER 12

REGION ONE

NORTHEAST

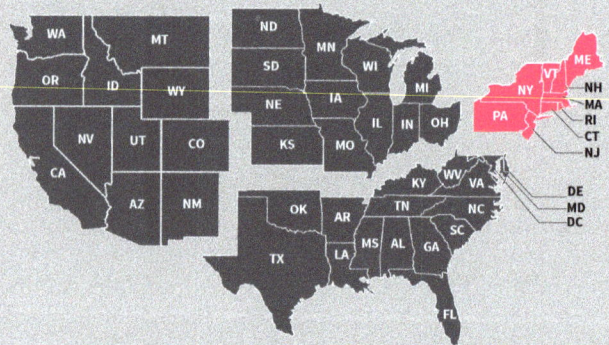

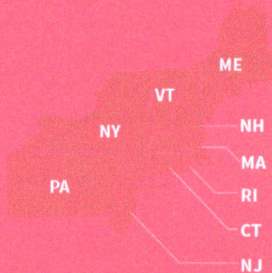

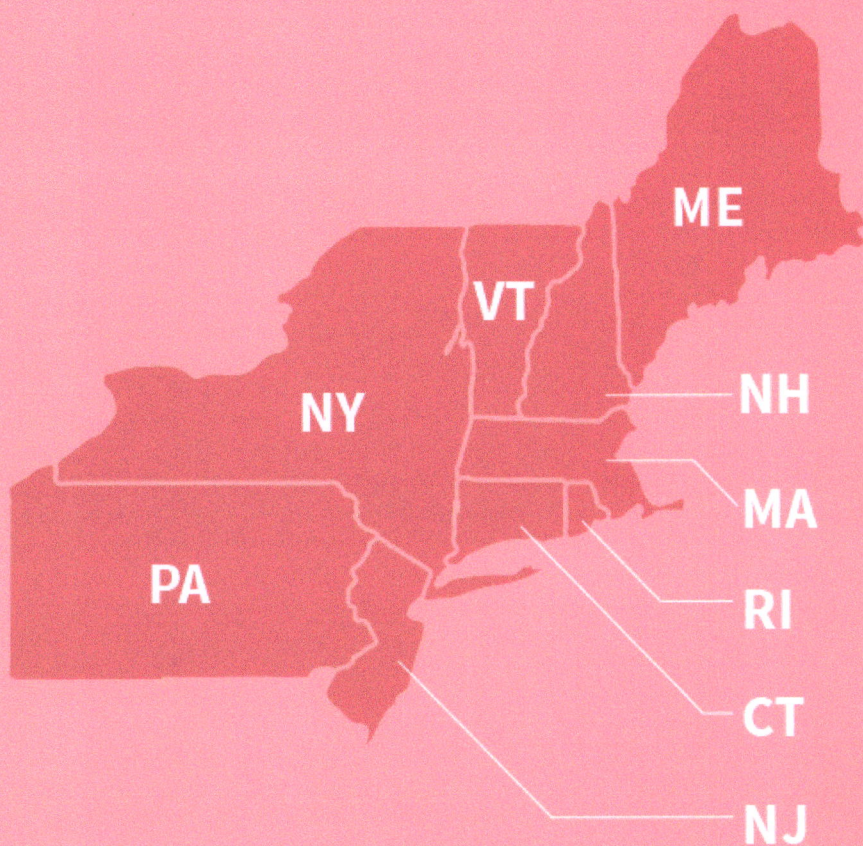

19 Programs | 9 States

1. CT - Yale University
2. MA - Boston University
3. MA - Massachusetts College of Art & Design
4. MA - University of Massachusetts, Dartmouth
5. NJ - Rutgers, The State University of New Jersey
6. NY - Alfred University
7. NY - Bard College
8. NY - Columbia University
9. NY - CUNY Hunter College
10. NY - Fashion Institute of Technology
11. NY - Parsons School of Design
12. NY - Pratt Institute
13. NY - Rochester Institute of Technology
14. NY - School of Visual Arts
15. NY - SUNY New Paltz
16. NY - Syracuse University
17. PA - Temple University
18. PA - University of the Arts
19. RI - Rhode Island School of Design

3D ART & DESIGN PROGRAMS

School	Avg. GPA, SAT Evidence-Based Reading Writing (ERW), SAT Math (M), and ACT Composite (C) Early Decision (ED): Yes/No	Admission Statistics	Program(s)	Portfolio Required (req.)
Yale University 220 York Street, Room 102, New Haven, CT 06511	GPA: N/A SAT (ERW): 720-780 SAT (M): 740-800 ACT (C): 33-35 ED: No, but Restrictive Early Action (REA) available	Overall College Admit Rate: 7% Undergrad Enrollment: 4,664 Total Enrollment: 12,060	BA Art, specialization: Sculpture	Portfolio not req.
Boston University 233 Bay State Road, Boston, MA 02215	GPA: 3.76 SAT (ERW): 640-720 SAT (M): 670-780 ACT (C): 30-34 ED: Yes	Overall College Admit Rate: 20% Undergrad Enrollment: 16,872 Total Enrollment: 32,718	BFA Sculpture	Portfolio req.
Massachusetts College of Art & Design 621 Huntington Ave, Boston, MA 02115	GPA: N/A SAT (ERW): N/A SAT (M): N/A ACT (C): N/A *Test-optional ED: No	Admit Rate: 70% Undergrad Enrollment: 1,770 Total Enrollment: 1,894	BFA Ceramics BFA Glass BFA Jewelry & Metalsmithing BFA Sculpture	Portfolio req.
University of Massachusetts, Dartmouth 285 Old Westport Rd, North Dartmouth, MA 02747	GPA: 3.31 SAT (ERW): 490-600 SAT (M): 500-590 ACT (C): 20-26 ED: No	Overall College Admit Rate: 76% Undergrad Enrollment: 6,027 Total Enrollment: 7,869	BFA Sculpture	Portfolio req.

School	Avg. GPA, SAT Evidence-Based Reading Writing (ERW), SAT Math (M), and ACT Composite (C) Early Decision (ED): Yes/No	Admission Statistics	Program(s)	Portfolio Required (req.)
Rutgers, The State University of New Jersey 100 Sutphen Road, Piscataway, NJ 08854	GPA: N/A SAT (ERW): 580-680 SAT (M): 600-730 ACT (C): 25-32 ED: No	Overall College Admit Rate: 67% Undergrad Enrollment: 35,844 Total Enrollment: 50,411	BFA Visual Arts, concentration: Sculpture	Portfolio req.
Alfred University 1 Saxon Dr, Alfred, NY 14802	GPA: 3.4 SAT (ERW): 480-600 SAT (M): 490-600 ACT (C): 21-27 ED: No	Overall College Admit Rate: 64% Undergrad Enrollment: 1,593 Total Enrollment: 2,187	BFA Art - Sculture/Dimensional Studies BFA Art - Ceramic Art	Portfolio req.
Bard College 30 Campus Road, Annandale-on-Hudson, NY 12504	GPA: N/A SAT (ERW): N/A* SAT (M): N/A* ACT (C): N/A* *Test-optional ED: Yes	Overall College Admit Rate: 57% Undergrad Enrollment: 2,118 Total Enrollment: 2,456	BA Studio Arts	Portfolio not req.
Columbia University 1130 Amsterdam Avenue, New York, NY 10027	GPA: N/A SAT (ERW): 720-770 SAT (M): 740-800 ACT (C): 33-35 ED: Yes	Overall College Admit Rate: 4% Undergrad Enrollment: 8,448 Total Enrollment: 31,455	BA Visual Arts, concentration: Sculpture	Portfolio not req.

NORTHEAST

3D ART & DESIGN PROGRAMS

School	Avg. GPA, SAT Evidence-Based Reading Writing (ERW), SAT Math (M), and ACT Composite (C) Early Decision (ED): Yes/No	Admission Statistics	Program(s)	Portfolio Required (req.)
CUNY Hunter College 695 Park Ave, New York, NY 10065	GPA: N/A SAT (ERW): 580-650 SAT (M): 590-690 ACT (C): 25-31 ED: No	Admit Rate: 40% Undergrad Enrollment: 17,943 Total Enrollment: 24,052	BFA Studio Art, concentration: Ceramics or Sculpture	Portfolio not req.
Fashion Institute of Technology (FIT) 227 West 27th Street, New York City, NY 10001	GPA: N/A SAT (ERW): N/A SAT (M): N/A ACT (C): N/A *FIT is test optional. ED: No	Admit Rate: 59% Undergrad Enrollment: 7,959 Total Enrollment: 8,191	AAS Jewelry Design BFA Packaging Design BFA Spatial Experience Design	Portfolio req.
Parsons - The New School 66 Fifth Avenue, New York, NY 10011	GPA: N/A SAT (ERW): 580-680 SAT (M): 560-680 ACT (C): 26-30 ED: No	Admit Rate: 69% Undergrad Enrollment: 6,399 Total Enrollment: 9,047	BFA Fine Arts	Portfolio req.
Pratt Institute 200 Willoughby Avenue, Brooklyn, NY 11205	GPA: 3.82 SAT (ERW): 570-660 SAT (M): 550-680 ACT (C): 25-30 ED: No	Admit Rate: 66% Undergrad Enrollment: 3,122 Total Enrollment: 4,353	BFA Fine Arts, emphases: Jewelry Sculpture & Integrated Practices	Portfolio req.

School	Avg. GPA, SAT Evidence-Based Reading Writing (ERW), SAT Math (M), and ACT Composite (C) Early Decision (ED): Yes/No	Admission Statistics	Program(s)	Portfolio Required (req.)
Rochester Institute of Technology 1 Lomb Memorial Dr, Rochester, NY 14623	GPA: 3.7 SAT (ERW): 600-690 SAT (M): 620-730 ACT (C): 28-33 ED: No	Overall College Admit Rate: 74% Undergrad Enrollment: 13,142 Total Enrollment: 16,158	BFA Studio Arts, options: Metals and Jewelry Design Ceramics Glass Sculpture	Portfolio req.
School of Visual Arts (SVA) 209 East 23rd Street, New York, NY 10010	GPA: 3.91 SAT (ERW): 545-650 SAT (M): 530-680 ACT (C): 23-27 ED: No	Overall College Admit Rate: 72% Undergrad Enrollment: 3,192 Total Enrollment: 3,692	BFA Fine Arts, concentration: Sculpture	Portfolio req.
SUNY New Paltz 1 Hawk Dr, New Paltz, NY 12561	GPA: 3.6 SAT (ERW): 530-630 SAT (M): 540-630 ACT (C): 24-29 ED: No	Admit Rate: 62% Undergrad Enrollment: 6,597 Total Enrollment: 7,489	BFA Ceramics BFA Metal BFA Sculpture	Portfolio req.
Syracuse University 401 University Place, Syracuse, NY 13244-2130	GPA: 3.67 SAT (ERW): N/A SAT (M): N/A ACT (C): N/A ED: Yes	Overall College Admit Rate: 69% Undergrad Enrollment: 14,479 Total Enrollment: 21,322	BFA Studio Arts, emphases: Ceramics Jewelry & Metalsmithing Sculpture Three Dimensional Studies	Portfolio req.

NORTHEAST

3D ART & DESIGN PROGRAMS

School	Avg. GPA, SAT Evidence-Based Reading Writing (ERW), SAT Math (M), and ACT Composite (C) Early Decision (ED): Yes/No	Admission Statistics	Program(s)	Portfolio Required (req.)
Temple University 1801 N Broad St, Philadelphia, PA 19122	GPA: 3.48 SAT (ERW): N/A* SAT (M): N/A* ACT (C): N/A* *Test-optional ED: No	Overall College Admit Rate: 71% Undergrad Enrollment: 27,306 Total Enrollment: 37,236	BFA Ceramics BFA Glass BFA Metals/Jewelry/ CAD-CAM BFA Sculpture	Portfolio req.
University of the Arts 320 S. Broad Street, Philadelphia, PA 19102	GPA: N/A SAT (ERW): N/A* SAT (M): N/A* ACT (C): N/A* *Test-optional ED: No	Overall College Admit Rate: 76% Undergrad Enrollment: 1,380 Total Enrollment: 1,530	BFA Fine Arts, concentration: Sculpture	Portfolio req.
Rhode Island School of Design (RISD) 2 College St, Providence, RI 02903	GPA: N/A SAT (ERW): 610-700 SAT (M): 640-770 ACT (C): 27-32 ED: Yes	Admit Rate: 27% Undergrad Enrollment: 1,736 Total Enrollment: 2,227	BFA Ceramics BFA Glass BFA Jewelry & Metalsmithing BFA Sculpture	Portfolio req.

CONNECTICUT

MAINE

MASSACHUSETTS

NEW HAMPSHIRE

NEW JERSEY

NEW YORK

PENNSYLVANIA

RHODE ISLAND

VERMONT

YALE UNIVERSITY

Address: 220 York Street, room 102, New Haven, CT 06511
Website: *https://www.art.yale.edu/about/study-areas/undergraduate-studies*
Contact: *https://www.yale.edu/contact-us*
Phone: (203) 432-4771
Email: student.questions@yale.edu

COST OF ATTENDANCE:

Tuition & Fees: $59,950 | **Additional Expenses:** $21,625
Total: $81,575

Financial Aid: https://www.yale.edu/admissions/financial-aid

ADDITIONAL INFORMATION:

Available Degree(s)

- BA Art, specialization: Sculpture

Portfolio Requirement

Portfolios are not required for incoming students. However, students must undergo the Sophomore Review as an undergraduate to continue on with the major. Applicants may submit an optional supplemental art portfolio.

Scholarships Offered

Yale scholarships are grants that are solely need-based. Merit-based scholarships are funded by external organizations or private companies. Yale does not require students, whose parents earn less than $65,000 annually, to contribute toward educational costs. Students whose families earn more than $150,000 may qualify for financial aid.

Special Opportunities

Art undergraduates at Yale are required to complete a senior project and participate in the Thesis Show, where they showcase their work. Art students are also in shared classrooms with Computing and the Arts majors. This major requires half of the coursework to be in computer science, and the other half in the arts.

Notable Alumni

Matthew Barney, Alex Da Corte, Eva Hesse, Nancy Graves, Wangechi Mutu, Charlotte Park, Martin Puryear, Frederic Remington, Priscilla Roberts, Fred Sandback, and Richard Serra

ME
VT
NY
NH
MA
PA
RI
CT
NJ

BOSTON UNIVERSITY

Address: 855 Commonwealth Avenue, Boston, MA 02215
Website: *https://www.bu.edu/cfa/academics/find-a-degreeprogram/school-of-visual-arts/sculpture/*
Contact: *https://www.bu.edu/about/contact-us/*
Phone: (617) 353-3350
Email: admissions@bu.edu

COST OF ATTENDANCE:

Tuition & Fees: $58,560 | **Additional Expenses:** $21,046
Total: $79,606

Financial Aid: http://www.bu.edu/finaid/

ADDITIONAL INFORMATION:

Available Degree(s)

- BFA Sculpture

Portfolio Requirement

Portfolios are required for incoming students. Submit 15-20 works via SlideRoom. At least three of the works must be created from observation.

Scholarships Offered

Boston University offers merit-based and need-based aid to all incoming students. Some of the merit scholarships for incoming students include the Trustee Scholarship (full tuition and fees), the Presidential Scholarship ($25,000 annually), the National Merit Scholarship (for National Merit finalists, valued at $25,000 per year), among many others. Need-based aid may come from the BU Grant, the BU Community Service Award, the Charles River Housing Grant, the Richard D. Cohen Scholarship (need and merit-based), or the Alumni Council Scholarship ($2,500).

Special Opportunities

Boston University's fine arts students must first complete the Foundation program. There, they take coursework in drawing, painting, and sculpture for their first two years. These foundational years focus on investigating materials and learning about the figure via observation. Sculpture students receive their own private studios in their third and fourth years. Electives include welding, ceramics, kinetic sculpture, and installation.

Notable Alumni

Penelope Jencks, Peter Schifrin, and Batu Siharulidze

CONNECTICUT

MAINE

MASSACHUSETTS

NEW HAMPSHIRE

NEW JERSEY

NEW YORK

PENNSYLVANIA

RHODE ISLAND

VERMONT

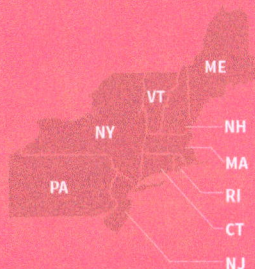

NORTHEAST

CONNECTICUT

MAINE

MASSACHUSETTS

NEW HAMPSHIRE

NEW JERSEY

NEW YORK

PENNSYLVANIA

RHODE ISLAND

VERMONT

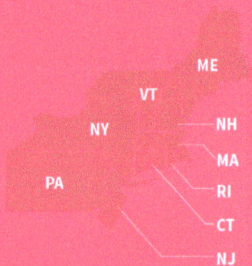

MASSACHUSETTS COLLEGE OF ART & DESIGN (MASSART)

Address: 621 Huntington Ave, Boston, MA 02115
Website: https://massart.edu/academics/programs
Contact: https://massart.edu/contactus
Phone: (617) 879-7000
Email: admissions@massart.edu

COST OF ATTENDANCE:

In-State Tuition & Fees: $14,200 | **Additional Expenses:** $19,200
Total: $33,400

New England Resident: $31,800 | **Additional Expenses:** $19,200
Total: $51,000

Out-of-State Tuition & Fees: $39,800 | **Additional Expenses:** $19,200
Total: $59,000

Financial Aid: https://massart.edu/financial-aid

ADDITIONAL INFORMATION:

Available Degree(s)

- BFA Ceramics
- BFA Glass
- BFA Jewelry & Metalsmithing
- BFA Sculpture

Portfolio Requirement
Portfolios are required for incoming students. Submit 15-20 examples of best and most recent work via the Common App. Applicants must not include artwork that copies another artist's work. Creative writing, screenplays, musical recordings, and theater performances are not allowed either.

Scholarships Offered
All eligible applicants are automatically considered for merit scholarships. To be considered, students need to demonstrate high academic achievement and showcase a strong portfolio. Out-of-state applicants may be eligible for the MassArt Merit Scholarship, the MassArt Transfer Merit Scholarship, or the Trustees Scholarship (covers all tuition and fees, renewable for four years). In-state applicants may be considered for the MassArt Merit Scholarship, the MassArt Transfer Merit Scholarship, and the Senator Paul E. Tsongas Scholarship (covers all tuition and fees for four years).

Special Opportunities
MassArt students have created a non-profit organization called Clay for Change. This organization raises money for various charities and local communities through selling their clay works. Glass students may be interested in the visiting artists that have worked directly with students to help them with their works, such as John drury and Robbie Miller. In the Jewelry major, students learn about techniques as well as exhibition and self-promotion strategies. Furthermore, Sculpture students have individual mentor time with faculty and group critiques.

Notable Alumni
Laura Brown, Rick Brown, Blane De St. Croix, Robert Cumming, Cyrus Edwin Dallin, Aimee Good, Luther Price, John Raimondi, and Jacqueline Winsor

UNIVERSITY OF MASSACHUSETTS, DARTMOUTH

Address: 285 Old Westport Rd, North Dartmouth, MA 02747
Website: *https://www.umassd.edu/programs/sculpture/*
Contact: *https://www.umassd.edu/undergraduate/contact/*
Phone: (508) 999-8703
Email: https://www.umassd.edu/undergraduate/contact/

COST OF ATTENDANCE:

In-State Tuition & Fees: $15,260 | **Additional Expenses:** $16,259
Total: $31,519

Out-of-State Tuition & Fees: $31,005 | **Additional Expenses:** $16,259
Total: $47,264

Financial Aid: https://www.umassd.edu/financialaid/

ADDITIONAL INFORMATION:

Available Degree(s)

- BFA Sculpture

Portfolio Requirement

Portfolios are required for incoming students. Submit 12 examples of best and most recent work via SlideRoom.

Scholarships Offered

All students are automatically considered for merit-based and need-based scholarships. UMass Dartmouth has scholarships such as the Chancellor's, Dean's, Admissions Award, Success, and the University Commonwealth Scholarships.

Special Opportunities

Students in the Sculpture program learn techniques such as welding, woodworking, mold-making, casting, and more. Internship opportunities are available and students are encouraged to apply. Ample work areas are available to all studio majors as well.

Notable Alumni

Bruce Gray, Susan Mohl Powers, and Bonnie Seeman

CONNECTICUT

MAINE

MASSACHUSETTS

NEW HAMPSHIRE

NEW JERSEY

NEW YORK

PENNSYLVANIA

RHODE ISLAND

VERMONT

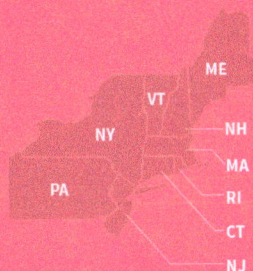

NORTHEAST

CONNECTICUT

MAINE

MASSACHUSETTS

NEW HAMPSHIRE

NEW JERSEY

NEW YORK

PENNSYLVANIA

RHODE ISLAND

VERMONT

RUTGERS, THE STATE UNIVERSITY OF NEW JERSEY

Address: 2 Chapel Drive, New Brunswick, NJ 08901
Website: *https://www.masongross.rutgers.edu/degrees-programs/art-design/programs/bfa/#visual-arts*
Contact: *https://www.masongross.rutgers.edu/admissions/contact*
Phone: (848) 932-5241
Email: admissions@ugadm.rutgers.edu

COST OF ATTENDANCE:

In-State Tuition & Fees: $16,010 | **Additional Expenses:** $20,257
Total: $36,267

Out-of-State Tuition & Fees: $33,082 | **Additional Expenses:** $20,769
Total: $53,851

Financial Aid: https://financialaid.rutgers.edu/

ADDITIONAL INFORMATION:

Available Degree(s)

- BFA Visual Arts, concentration: Sculpture

Portfolio Requirement

Portfolios are required for incoming students, for both degrees. Submit 15-20 works created within the past two years. Include at least one sketchbook page and a variety of media, such as observational drawings, paintings, print, or sculpture.

Scholarships Offered

Scholarships are awarded on a rolling basis, based on fund availability.

Special Opportunities

Students in the BFA Visual Arts program have six concentrations to choose from. They must complete three, year-long studio courses and complete seminars within their chosen area. Their concentration may be declared at their sophomore review. Students may do a double or hybrid concentration with faculty approval.

Notable Alumni

Brad Ascalon, Alice Aycock, Marc Ecko, Lore Kadden Lindenfeld, Kojiro Matsukata, and George Segal

ALFRED UNIVERSITY

Address: 1 Saxon Dr, Alfred, NY 14802
Website: *https://www.alfred.edu/academics/undergrad-majors-minors/art-sculpture-dimensional.cfm*
Contact: *https://www.alfred.edu/about/contact.cfm*
Phone: (607) 871-2115
Email: admissions@alfredstate.edu

COST OF ATTENDANCE:

Tuition & Fees: $22,448 | **Additional Expenses:** $16,902
Total: $39,350

Financial Aid: https://www.alfred.edu/admissions/financial-aid/

ADDITIONAL INFORMATION:

Available Degree(s)

- BFA Art - Sculture/Dimensional Studies
- BFA Art - Ceramic Art

Portfolio Requirement

Portfolios are required for incoming students. Submit 15-20 examples of best and most recent work via the SlideRoom. Four works must be from direct observation.

Scholarships Offered

According to Alfred University, "every accepted student will receive at least 50% off tuition." They offer merit-based and need-based scholarships to incoming students. New York State residents automatically receive up to $25,000 towards their cost of attendance. Art portfolio awards are also available.

Special Opportunities

Students in the Sculpture/Dimensional studies program learn techniques in glass sculpture, neon work, wood, metal, and more. The major is grounded in material tradition and promoting creative study. Students in the Ceramics program learn clay making, glaze formulation, throwing, kiln loading, slip-casting, and more. In the senior year, Ceramic students work one-on-one with a faculty advisor in an assigned personal studio.

Notable Alumni

Jerry Ackerman, Robert Archambeau, Arthur Eugene Baggs, R. Guy Cowan, Andrew Deutsch, Ken Ferguson, Rob Forbes, Julia Galloway, Maijia Grotell, Vivika Heino, Ka Kwong Hui, Jae Won Lee, Charles Loloma, Otellie Loloma, Kristen Morgin, Kenneth Price, Daniel Rhodes, Adelaïde Alsop Robineau, Annabeth Rosen, Siona Shimshi, Robert C. Turner, Betty Woodman, and Arnold Zimmerman

CONNECTICUT

MAINE

MASSACHUSETTS

NEW HAMPSHIRE

NEW JERSEY

NEW YORK

PENNSYLVANIA

RHODE ISLAND

VERMONT

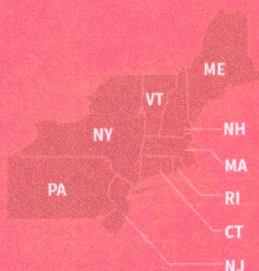

NORTHEAST

CONNECTICUT

MAINE

MASSACHUSETTS

NEW HAMPSHIRE

NEW JERSEY

NEW YORK

PENNSYLVANIA

RHODE ISLAND

VERMONT

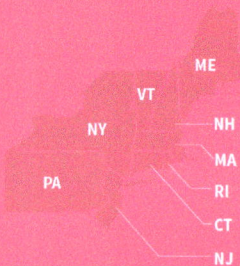

BARD COLLEGE

Address: 30 Campus Road, Annandale-on-Hudson, NY 12504
Website: *https://studioarts.bard.edu/*
Contact: *https://www.bard.edu/admission/contact/*
Phone: (845) 758-7472
Email: admissions@bard.edu

COST OF ATTENDANCE:

Tuition & Fees: $57,498 | **Additional Expenses:** $17,455
Total: $74,953

Financial Aid: https://www.bard.edu/financialaid/

ADDITIONAL INFORMATION:

Available Degree(s)

- BA Studio Arts

Portfolio Requirement

Portfolios are not required for incoming students. However, there is an optional supplemental submission.

Scholarships Offered

All scholarships at Bard are merit-based and need-based. Students are automatically considered for these rewards when they submit their university application. Scholarships include the Civic Engagement Scholarship, the President's Scholarship, the Bard Scholarship, and more.

Special Opportunities

At the end of the second year, students must present their work to a panel of faculty judges that will critique the student's body of work thus far. After passing the moderation process, students may take Level III coursework in advanced painting, drawing, sculpture, installation, and printmaking techniques. Seniors must complete a senior project and present their work at an open exhibition.

Notable Alumni

Robert C. Bassler, Sadie Benning, Cecilia Berkovic, Nayland Blake, Paul Chan, Ronald Chase, Frances Bean Cobain, Adriana Farmiga, Joanne Greenbaum, Daniel Gordon, David Horvitz, Jamie Livingston, Mary Lum, Malerie Marder, Lothar Osterburg, Serkan Ozkaya, R.H. Quaytman, Kristin Schattenfield-Rein, Carolee Schneeman, Amy Sillman Xaviera Simmons, Gordon Stevenson, and Rudi Stern

COLUMBIA UNIVERSITY

Address: 1130 Amsterdam Avenue, New York, NY 10027
Website: *https://arts.columbia.edu/undergraduate-visual-arts-program*
Contact: *https://undergrad.admissions.columbia.edu/contact*
Phone: (212) 854-2522
Email: ugrad-ask@columbia.edu

COST OF ATTENDANCE:

Tuition & Fees: $63,530 | **Additional Expenses:** $19,054
Total: $82,584

Financial Aid: https://www.sfs.columbia.edu/fin-aid

ADDITIONAL INFORMATION:

Available Degree(s)

- BA Visual Arts, concentration: Sculpture

Portfolio Requirement

Portfolios are not required for incoming students. However, Columbia accepts optional creative supplements.

Scholarships Offered

Columbia University offers need-based aid. They also offer fellowships to students from specific backgrounds.

Special Opportunities

The Visual Arts program at Columbia is interdisciplinary. Students explore various forms of visual expression. They also learn techniques while enhancing their analytical voice. Undergraduates in this program may choose a concentration in Drawing, Painting, Sculpture, Photography, Printmaking, or Video. They may combine any of these disciplines as well.

Notable Alumni

Helaine Blumenfeld, Leroy Lamis, Isamu Noguchi, and George Wyatt

CONNECTICUT

MAINE

MASSACHUSETTS

NEW HAMPSHIRE

NEW JERSEY

NEW YORK

PENNSYLVANIA

RHODE ISLAND

VERMONT

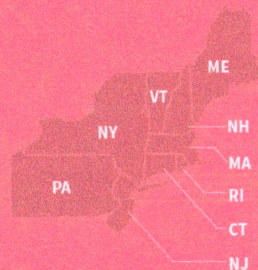

NORTHEAST

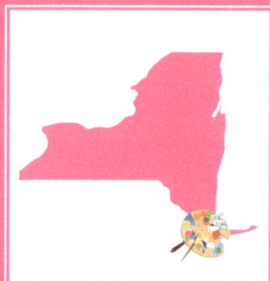

CONNECTICUT

MAINE

MASSACHUSETTS

NEW HAMPSHIRE

NEW JERSEY

NEW YORK

PENNSYLVANIA

RHODE ISLAND

VERMONT

CUNY HUNTER COLLEGE

Address: 695 Park Ave, New York, NY 10065
Website: *https://huntercollegeart.org/bfa-program/*
Contact: *http://www.hunter.cuny.edu/admissions/undergraduateadmissions/contactus*
Phone: (212) 772-4490
Email: admissions@hunter.cuny.edu

COST OF ATTENDANCE:

In-State Tuition & Fees: $6,930 | **Additional Expenses:** $20,478
Total: $27,408

Out-of-State Tuition & Fees: $18,600 | **Additional Expenses:** $20,478
Total: $39,078

Financial Aid: https://hunter.cuny.edu/students/financial-aid/

ADDITIONAL INFORMATION:

Available Degree(s)

- BFA Studio Art, concentration: Ceramics or Sculpture

Portfolio Requirement

Portfolios are not required for incoming students. However they may be at some point along the BFA program.

Scholarships Offered

CUNY Hunter College offers the Guttman Transfer Scholarships and the William E. Macaulay Honors Program. Students must complete the FAFSA to be considered for these scholarships. Hunter College students may also apply for applications such as the Freshman Honors Scholar Program, International Student Scholarships, and more. A FAFSA is required each year.

Special Opportunities

The CUNY Hunter BFA program is a fifth-year program, meaning that it takes, on average, five years to complete. The extra year is meant to serve as an opportunity for an in-depth focus into studio practice, contemporary art, and theoretical issues. The program culminates in a BFA Degree Show. Students learn about all phases of creating an exhibition, and are involved in tasks such as lighting, labeling, designing, installation, planning, and scheduling the event.

Notable Alumni

Firelei Baez, Jules de Balincourt, Jacqueline Donachie, Mel Kendrick, Terrance Lindall, Robert Morris, and Brian Wood

ME
VT
NY
NH
MA
PA
RI
CT
NJ

FASHION INSTITUTE OF TECHNOLOGY (FIT)

Address: 227 West 27th Street, New York City, NY 10001
Website: *https://www.fitnyc.edu/academics/academic-divisions/art-and-design/jewelry-design/index.php*
Contact: *http://www.fitnyc.edu/about/contact/index.php*
Phone: (212) 217-3760
Email: fitinfo@fitnyc.edu

COST OF ATTENDANCE:

In-State Tuition & Fees: $7,920 | **Additional Expenses:** $18,556
Total: $26,476

Out-of-State Tuition & Fees: $22,242 | **Additional Expenses:** $18,556
Total: $40,798

Financial Aid: https://www.fitnyc.edu/admissions/costs/financial-aid/index.php

ADDITIONAL INFORMATION:

Available Degree(s)

- AAS Jewelry Design
- BFA Spatial Experience Design
- BFA Packaging Design

Portfolio Requirement

At FIT, high school applicants must apply to an AAS program first. After successful completion of the AAS degree, they may then apply for a BFA program. Portfolios are required for incoming students. The AAS in Jewelry Design requires a written essay and portfolio of 10-15 works. At least 5-7 works must contain drawings from observation and an additional 3-5 must include jewelry pieces drawn to scale.

Scholarships Offered

FIT scholarships are donor scholarships typically gifted to students with high financial need. The average award is $1,100.

Special Opportunities

The two-year jewelry design program integrates craftsmanship, digital literacy, and business practices. Students learn principles of production methods, how to utilize CAD and 3D modeling, 3D printing, CNC milling, the study of gems and more.

Notable Alumni

Leslie Blodgett, Fran Boller, Jesse Carrier, Tony Chi, David Chu, Dorothy Cosonas, Laverne Cox, Randy Fenoli, William Frake, Nina Garcia, Zaldy Goco, Norma Kamali, Calvin Klein, Michael Kors, Raymond Matts, Luke Meier, Edward Menicheschi, Mara Miller, Bibhu Mohapatra, Robert Rodriguez, Daniel Roseberry, Ivy Ross, James Rothwell, Ralph Rucci, Stephen A. Smith, Suzanne Tick, and David Voss

CONNECTICUT

MAINE

MASSACHUSETTS

NEW HAMPSHIRE

NEW JERSEY

NEW YORK

PENNSYLVANIA

RHODE ISLAND

VERMONT

NORTHEAST

CONNECTICUT

MAINE

MASSACHUSETTS

NEW HAMPSHIRE

NEW JERSEY

NEW YORK

PENNSYLVANIA

RHODE ISLAND

VERMONT

PARSONS - THE NEW SCHOOL

Address: 66 Fifth Avenue, New York, NY 10011
Website: *https://www.newschool.edu/parsons/bfa-fine-arts/*
Contact: *https://www.newschool.edu/parsons/contact/*
Phone: (212) 229-8900
Email: thinkparsons@newschool.edu

COST OF ATTENDANCE:

Tuition & Fees: $51,722 | **Additional Expenses:** N/A
Total: $51,722

Financial Aid: https://www.newschool.edu/financial-aid/

ADDITIONAL INFORMATION:

Available Degree(s)

- BFA Fine Arts

Portfolio Requirement

Portfolios are required for incoming students. Applicants must complete the Parsons Challenge, a new visual work inspired by a theme set by the university. Applicants must also submit 8-12 works. Submit via SlideRoom.

Scholarships Offered

The New School offers merit-based and need-based aid to students. Students are automatically considered for merit-based scholarships. These are based on the strength of the application and portfolio. Need-based aid is available to students who are eligible and submit the FAFSA.

Special Opportunities

BFA Fine Arts students at Parsons study painting, drawing, sculpture, and 4D media. They also have access and proximity to museums, art galleries, internships, and other opportunities to engage with artists and network. Students are encouraged to study abroad to gain new perspectives. Study abroad opportunities are in Paris, London, Florence, and more.

Notable Alumni

Kevin Appel, Rosemary Cove, Jane Frank, Adolph Gottlieb, Julie Harvey, Edward Hopper, Steffani Jemison, Jasper Johns, Shirley Kaneda, Sol Kjok, Dimitar Lukanov, Rob Pruitt, Andrew Cornell Robinson, Norman Rockwell, Anrika Rupp, Gavin Spielman, Emily Sundblad, Rodel Tapaya, Julie Umerle, Nick van Woert, Betsy Wolfston, Ai Weiwei, and Janise Yntema

PRATT INSTITUTE

Address: 200 Willoughby Avenue, Brooklyn, NY 11205
Website: *https://www.pratt.edu/academics/school-of-art/ undergraduate-school-of-art/undergraduate-fine-arts/finearts-areas/*
Contact: *https://www.pratt.edu/academics/school-of-design/ undergraduate-school-of-design/fashion/fashion-department- contact/*
Phone: (718) 636-3600

Email: admissions@pratt.edu

COST OF ATTENDANCE:

Tuition & Fees: $53,566 | **Additional Expenses:** $19,824
Total: $73,390

Financial Aid: https://www.pratt.edu/admissions/financing-your- education/financing-undergraduate/

ADDITIONAL INFORMATION:

Available Degree(s)

- BFA Fine Arts, emphasis: Jewelry or Sculpture & Integrated Practices

Portfolio Requirement

Portfolios are required for incoming students. Submit 12-20 drawings of your most recent work. Students must include 3-5 drawings from observation. Submit via SlideRoom.

Scholarships Offered

Pratt offers merit-based and endowed scholarships in addition to need-based grants. Furthermore, there are merit-based scholarships available to international students as well. The Presidential Merit- Based Scholarships are available to all Pratt students in varied award amounts.

Special Opportunities

In the first year, Fine Arts students take foundational studio coursework and liberal arts classes. In the second year, students continue with liberal arts coursework and start taking courses more focused in their areas of emphasis. Electives are taken in the third and fourth years. Examples of available electives include charcoal drawing, bronze casting, etching and ceramics, new media, and more. The program culminates in a thesis and an exhibition of their work on campus.

Notable Alumni

Louise Abel, Tina Allen, David Ascalon, Xenobia Bailey, Lilian Thomas Burwell, Jay Hall Carpenter, Aurore Chabot, Donna Chambers, Tom Cramer, and William R. Cumpiano

CONNECTICUT

MAINE

MASSACHUSETTS

NEW HAMPSHIRE

NEW JERSEY

NEW YORK

PENNSYLVANIA

RHODE ISLAND

VERMONT

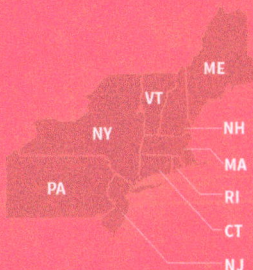

NORTHEAST

CONNECTICUT

MAINE

MASSACHUSETTS

NEW HAMPSHIRE

NEW JERSEY

NEW YORK

PENNSYLVANIA

RHODE ISLAND

VERMONT

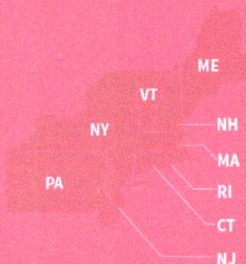

ROCHESTER INSTITUTE OF TECHNOLOGY

Address: 209 East 23rd Street, New York, NY 10010
Website: *https://www.rit.edu/artdesign/study/studio-arts-bfa*
Contact: *https://www.rit.edu/admissions/contacts*
Phone: (585) 475-6631
Email: admissions@rit.edu

COST OF ATTENDANCE:

Tuition & Fees: $54,058 | **Additional Expenses:** $18,296
Total: $72,354

Financial Aid: https://www.rit.edu/admissions/financial-aid

ADDITIONAL INFORMATION:

Available Degree(s)

- BFA Studio Arts, option: Metals and Jewelry Design, Ceramics, Glass, or Sculpture

Portfolio Requirement

Portfolios are required for incoming students. Submit up to 20 of your best and most recent works via SlideRoom.

Scholarships Offered

All applicants are considered for merit-based scholarships upon submission of their application. No separate application is required. RIT also offers numerous merit-based and need-based scholarships for students from different backgrounds or different majors.

Special Opportunities

RIT offers cooperative education and internships with top companies, Students gain real-world career experience prior to graduation. Seniors in the BFA Studio Arts program are required to complete a senior art exhibition. Students may choose from coursework such as Business Practices for Artists, Mold Mechanisms, 4D Design, Furniture Design, Molten Glass Practice, and more.

Notable Alumni

Mike Battle, Kei Ito, Mary Lum, Elli Perkins, and Junco Sato Pollack

SCHOOL OF VISUAL ARTS (SVA)

Address: 209 East 23rd Street, New York, NY 10010
Website: *https://sva.edu/academics/undergraduate/bfa-fine-arts*
Contact: *https://sva.edu/contact-and-map*
Phone: (212) 592- 2100
Email: admissions@sva.edu

COST OF ATTENDANCE:

Tuition & Fees: $49,750 | **Additional Expenses:** N/A
Total: $49,750

Financial Aid: https://sva.edu/admissions/financial-resources/
financial-aid

ADDITIONAL INFORMATION:

Available Degree(s)

- BFA Fine Arts, concentration: Sculpture

Portfolio Requirement

Portfolios are required for incoming students. Submit 15-20 works
via SlideRoom.

Scholarships Offered

The Silad H. Rhodes Scholarship is available to students of all
majors with an unlisted award amount. Students with a GPA of
3.0+ are eligible. First-time freshmen applicants must submit all
application materials by February to be considered. There is no
separate application.

Special Opportunities

SVA is located within walking distance of many world-famous
museums and galleries. Facilities include wood and metal shops,
ceramics, the Fine Arts Bio Art Lab, a printmaking lab, as well as
sound and fibers studios. Seniors showcase their artwork at Open
Studios, which dealers and curators attend. It is an opportunity
for students to network with professionals in the field. Off-site
workshops are also held in metal casting, neon, glass-making, and
large-scale ceramics.

Notable Alumni

Kesewa Aboah, Esao Andrews, Ali Banisadr, Samuel Bayer, Robert
Beauchamp, Tom Burr, Robin Byrd, Rosson Crow, Inka Essenhigh,
Neck Face, Charles Fazzino, Andrea Fraser, Pamela Fraser, Barnaby
Furnas, Jedd Garet, Rita Genet, Kate Gilmore, Keith Haring, Jane
hart, gus Heinze, Reverend Jen, Vashtie Kola, Joseph Kosuth, Tina La
Porta, Robert Lazzarini, Dinh Q. Lê, Sol LeWitt, Jennifer Macdonald,
Donald Martiny, Mark McCoy, Aleksandra Mir, Steve Mumford, Paul
A. Paddock, Elizabeth Peyton, Andrew Cornell Robinson, Jorge Luis
Rodriguez, Brian Rutenberg, Kenny Scharf, Jeff Sonhouse, Sarah
Sze, John von Bergen, and Charlie White

CONNECTICUT

MAINE

MASSACHUSETTS

NEW HAMPSHIRE

NEW JERSEY

NEW YORK

PENNSYLVANIA

RHODE ISLAND

VERMONT

NORTHEAST

CONNECTICUT

MAINE

MASSACHUSETTS

NEW HAMPSHIRE

NEW JERSEY

NEW YORK

PENNSYLVANIA

RHODE ISLAND

VERMONT

SUNY NEW PALTZ

Address: 1 Hawk Dr, New Paltz, NY 12561
Website: *https://www.newpaltz.edu/fpa/art/*
Contact: *https://www.newpaltz.edu/admissions/contact.html*
Phone: (845) 257-3200
Email: admissions@newpaltz.edu

COST OF ATTENDANCE:

In-State Tuition & Fees: $8,502 | **Additional Expenses:** $17,728
Total: $26,230

Out-of-State Tuition & Fees: $18,412 | **Additional Expenses:** $17,728
Total: $36,140

Financial Aid: https://www.newpaltz.edu/financialaid/

ADDITIONAL INFORMATION:

Available Degree(s)

- BFA Ceramics
- BFA Metal
- BFA Sculpture

Portfolio Requirement

Portfolios are required for incoming students. Submit 12 of your strongest works.

Scholarships Offered

SUNY New Paltz encourages students to apply for external and private scholarships. The university also has a scholarship portal for students to find and apply directly to scholarships.

Special Opportunities

Suny New Paltz's proximity to New York City allows students the opportunity to obtain various internship opportunities, access to special events, and field trips. The campus houses well-equipped studios for ceramic fabrication, studio space, metalworking equipment, and more.

Notable Alumni

Marco Dasilva and Marco Maggi

SYRACUSE UNIVERSITY

Address: 202 Crouse College, Syracuse, NY 13244
Website: *https://vpa.syr.edu/academics/art/programs/studio-arts-bfa/*
Contact: *https://www.syracuse.edu/admissions/undergraduate/contact/*
Phone: (315) 443-2769
Email: admissu@syr.edu

COST OF ATTENDANCE:

Tuition & Fees: $57,591 | **Additional Expenses:** $44,448.8
Total: $80,039.80

Financial Aid: https://www.syracuse.edu/admissions/cost-and-aid/

ADDITIONAL INFORMATION:

Available Degree(s)

- BFA Studio Arts, emphasis: Ceramics, Jewelry & Metalsmithing, Sculpture, or Three Dimensional Studies

Portfolio Requirement

Portfolios are required for incoming students. Submit 12-20 recent works. Syracuse University strongly suggests that at least six drawings are from observation.

Scholarships Offered

Syracuse University offers various merit-based and need-based scholarships and grants. The 1870 Scholarship covers full tuition for the full length of the undergraduate program. Artistic Scholarships are awarded to students based on talent and a maintained cumulative GPA of 2.75+.

Special Opportunities

Syracuse University offers the VPA Study Abroad experience for art majors. Studio Art majors frequently go to Florence, Italy for their study abroad experience.

Notable Alumni

Elfriede Abbe, Gordon Chandler, Sol LeWitt, Ivan Meštrović, and Jim Ridlon

CONNECTICUT

MAINE

MASSACHUSETTS

NEW HAMPSHIRE

NEW JERSEY

NEW YORK

PENNSYLVANIA

RHODE ISLAND

VERMONT

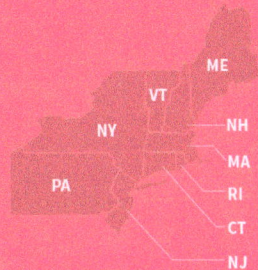

NORTHEAST

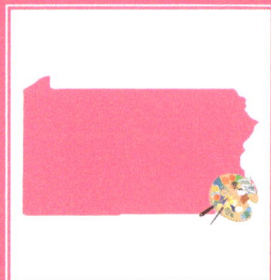

TEMPLE UNIVERSITY

Address: 1801 N Broad St, Philadelphia, PA 19122
Website: *https://tyler.temple.edu/academic-programs*
Contact: *https://www.temple.edu/contact/*
Phone: (215) 204-7000
Email: askanowl@temple.edu

COST OF ATTENDANCE:

In-State Tuition & Fees: $18,168 | **Additional Expenses:** $17,880
Total: $36,048

Out-of-State Tuition & Fees: $31,440 | **Additional Expenses:** $19,944
Total: $51,384

Financial Aid: https://admissions.temple.edu/costs-aid-scholarships/financial-aid-scholarships

ADDITIONAL INFORMATION:

Available Degree(s)

- BFA Ceramics
- BFA Glass
- BFA Metals/Jewelry/CAD-CAM
- BFA Sculpture

Portfolio Requirement

Portfolios are required for incoming students. Submit via SlideRoom.

Scholarships Offered

All students who submit their application by February 1 are automatically considered for merit scholarships. Award amounts range from $1,000 to full tuition.

Special Opportunities

Students have access to numerous kilns, a glaze room, an 18-station throwing studio, space for large-scale installations, and 10,000 square feet of spaces for ceramics students. Metals/Jewelry students have 6,000 square feet devoted to 3D printing, jewelry-making, and metalsmithing. Students have access to a state-of-the-art 3D printing lab and an electroforming lab. Glass students have a 10,000 square foot space devoted solely to glass. The hot shop has 530-pound day tanks, 10 dedicated annealers, and more. Last, sculpture students have access to over 16,000 square feet of studio space, including a woodshop, metal fabrication shop, and mold-making facilities.

Notable Alumni

Laura Marie Greenwood, Trenton Doyle Hancock, Andrew Hussie, Simmie Knox, Nicholas Muellner, Ralph Rucci, Paula Scher, Sarai Sherman, Aaron Shikler, and Jen Simmons

CONNECTICUT

MAINE

MASSACHUSETTS

NEW HAMPSHIRE

NEW JERSEY

NEW YORK

PENNSYLVANIA

RHODE ISLAND

VERMONT

UNIVERSITY OF THE ARTS

Address: 320 S. Broad Street, Philadelphia, PA 19102
Website: *https://www.uarts.edu/academics/school-art/IFA/sculpture*
Contact: *https://www.uarts.edu/about/contact-us*
Phone: (215) 717-6049
Email: admissions@uarts.edu

COST OF ATTENDANCE:

Tuition & Fees: $48,350 | **Additional Expenses:** $20,600
Total: $68,950

Financial Aid: https://www.uarts.edu/tuition-and-financial-aid

ADDITIONAL INFORMATION:

Available Degree(s)

- BFA Fine Arts, concentration: Sculpture

Portfolio Requirement

Portfolios are required for incoming students. Submit 15-20 examples of work within the past two years.

Scholarships Offered

Various named scholarships are available to all students for varied award amounts. Some scholarships are available to all University of the Arts students, such as the W.W. Smith Scholarship, the James M. Cresson, Scholarship, the Arnold A. Bayard Scholarship, and more.

Special Opportunities

Students in the Sculpture concentration learn the basic disciplines within Painting and Expanded Drawing and dive into the expanded field of sculpture as well. Juniors and seniors focus on independently-driven projects derived from their own research.

Notable Alumni

Meta Vaux Warrick Fuller, Marshall K. Harris, Joseph Menna, Flo Perkins, and Samuel Yellin

CONNECTICUT

MAINE

MASSACHUSETTS

NEW HAMPSHIRE

NEW JERSEY

NEW YORK

PENNSYLVANIA

RHODE ISLAND

VERMONT

NORTHEAST

CONNECTICUT

MAINE

MASSACHUSETTS

NEW HAMPSHIRE

NEW JERSEY

NEW YORK

PENNSYLVANIA

RHODE ISLAND

VERMONT

RHODE ISLAND SCHOOL OF DESIGN (RISD)

Address: 2 College St, Providence, RI 02903
Website: *https://www.risd.edu/academics/undergraduate-study*
Contact: *https://www.risd.edu/about/contact*
Phone: (401) 454-6300
Email: admissions@risd.edu

COST OF ATTENDANCE:

Tuition & Fees: $55,220 | **Additional Expenses:** $22,060
Total: $77,280

Financial Aid: https://www.risd.edu/student-financial-services/
undergraduate-aid/

ADDITIONAL INFORMATION:

Available Degree(s)

- BFA Ceramics
- BFA Glass
- BFA Jewelry & Metalsmithing
- BFA Sculpture

Portfolio Requirement

Portfolios are required for incoming students. Submit 12-20 recent
works via SlideRoom. Applicants are strongly encouraged to submit
drawings from observation. Applicants must also complete The
Assignment - a two-part portfolio requirement that involves a visual
study based on a prompt.

Scholarships Offered

RISD scholarships are need-based. Students must submit a FAFSA
application each year to be considered. RISD is also partnered with
Scholarship Universe, a website that matches students with outside
scholarships and keeps students on track with deadlines.

Special Opportunities

The RISD Museum is located next door for easy access to a collection
of painting and sculpture from almost every period and global
works. Students also have access to specimens in the Nature Lab.

Notable Alumni

Frederick Warren Allen, Janine Antoni, Tanya Aguiñiga, Howard Ben
Tré, John Benson, Huma Bhabha, James Carpenter, Otto Heino,
Vivika Heino, Karen LaMonte, Ross Palmer Beecher, and John Prip

ME
VT
NY
NH
MA
PA
RI
CT
NJ

CHAPTER 13

REGION TWO

MIDWEST

ILLINOIS

INDIANA

IOWA

KANSAS

MICHIGAN

MINNESOTA

MISSOURI

NEBRASKA

NORTH DAKOTA

OHIO

SOUTH DAKOTA

WISCONSIN

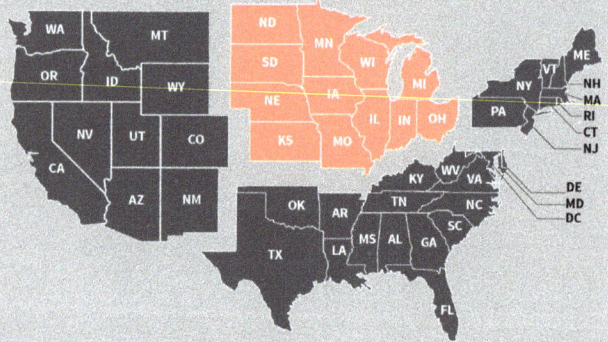

10 *Programs* | 12 *States*

1. IL - School of the Art Institute Chicago
2. IL - University of Illinois, Urbana-Champaign
3. IN - Indiana University Bloomington
4. KS - University of Kansas
5. MI - College for Creative Studies
6. MI - University of Michigan
7. OH - Cleveland Institute of Art
8. OH - Columbus College of Art & Design
9. OH - Ohio State University
10. WI - University of Wisconsin, Madison

3D ART & DESIGN PROGRAMS

School	Avg. GPA, SAT Evidence-Based Reading Writing (ERW), SAT Math (M), and ACT Composite (C) Early Decision (ED): Yes/No	Admission Statistics	Program(s)	Portfolio Required (req.)
School of the Art Institute of Chicago (SAIC) 36 S. Wabash Ave., Chicago, IL 60603	GPA: N/A SAT (ERW): 560-660 SAT (M): 480-600 ACT (C): 22-25 ED: No	Admit Rate: 78% Undergrad Enrollment: 2,487 Total Enrollment: 3,132	BFA Studio, areas: Ceramics Sculpture	Portfolio req.
University of Illinois Urbana-Champaign (UIUC) 901 West Illinois Street, Urbana, IL 61801	GPA: N/A SAT (ERW): 590-700 SAT (M): 620-770 ACT (C): 27-33 ED: Yes	Overall College Admit Rate: 50% Undergrad Enrollment: 34,559 Total Enrollment: 56,257	BA Studio Art, concentration: Sculpture BFA Studio Art, concentration: Sculpture	Portfolio req.
Indiana University Bloomington 107 S. Indiana Avenue, Bloomington, IN 47405	GPA: 3.74 SAT (ERW): 580-700 SAT (M): 560-680 ACT (C): 26-32 ED: No	Overall College Admit Rate: 85% Undergrad Enrollment: 34,253 Total Enrollment: 45,328	BFA Studio Art, concentration: Ceramics, Metals + Jewelry, Sculpture	Portfolio not req.
University of Kansas 1502 Iowa St., Lawrence, KS 66045	GPA: 3.66 SAT (ERW): 550-660 SAT (M): 540-670 ACT (C): 21-29 ED: No	Overall College Admit Rate: 92% Undergrad Enrollment: 19,158 Total Enrollment: 26,780	BFA Ceramics BFA Metalsmith-ing/Jewelry BFA Visual Art BA Visual Art	Portfolio req.

School	Avg. GPA, SAT Evidence-Based Reading Writing (ERW), SAT Math (M), and ACT Composite (C) Early Decision (ED): Yes/No	Admission Statistics	Program(s)	Portfolio Required (req.)
College for Creative Studies 201 E. Kirby, Detroit, MI 48202	GPA: N/A SAT (ERW): N/A* SAT (M): N/A* ACT (C): N/A* *Not required nor accepted ED: No	Overall College Admit Rate: 55% Undergrad Enrollment: 1,462 Total Enrollment: 1,512	BFA Craft and Material Studies	Portfolio req.
University of Michigan 500 S. State St., Ann Arbor, MI 48109	GPA: 3.87 SAT (ERW): 660-740 SAT (M): 680-780 ACT (C): 31-34 ED: No	Overall College Admit Rate: 26% Undergrad Enrollment: 31,329 Total Enrollment: 47,907	BFA Art & Design	Portfolio req.
Cleveland Institute of Art 11610 Euclid Avenue, Cleveland, OH 44106	GPA: N/A SAT (ERW): 560-680 SAT (M): 510-620 ACT (C): 19-27 ED: No	Overall College Admit Rate: 67% Undergrad Enrollment: 599 Total Enrollment: 599	BFA Craft & Design BFA Sculpture & Expanded Media	Portfolio req.
Columbus College of Art and Design 60 Cleveland Ave, Columbus, OH 43215	GPA: N/A SAT (ERW): N/A SAT (M): N/A ACT (C): N/A *Test-optional ED: No	Admit Rate: 92% Undergrad Enrollment: 982 Total Enrollment: 1,009	BFA Fine Arts, concentrations: Ceramics Glass Jewelry Sculpture	Portfolio req.

MIDWEST

3D ART & DESIGN PROGRAMS

School	Avg. GPA, SAT Evidence-Based Reading Writing (ERW), SAT Math (M), and ACT Composite (C) Early Decision (ED): Yes/No	Admission Statistics	Program(s)	Portfolio Required (req.)
Ohio State University 1849 Cannon Drive, Columbus, OH 43210	GPA: N/A SAT (ERW): 590-690 SAT (M): 620-740 ACT (C): 26-32 ED: No	Overall College Admit Rate: 87% Undergrad Enrollment: 19,284 Total Enrollment: 25,714	BFA Art, emphases: Ceramics Glass Sculpture	Portfolio not req.
University of Wisconsin 702 West Johnson Street, Madison, WI 53715	GPA: 3.87 SAT (ERW): 610-690 SAT (M): 650-770 ACT (C): 27-32 ED: No	Overall College Admit Rate: 57% Undergrad Enrollment: 32,688 Total Enrollment: 44,640	BFA Art, concentration: Contemporary 3D Practices	Portfolio not req.

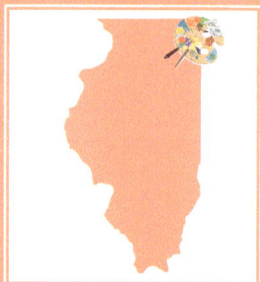

ILLINOIS

INDIANA

IOWA

KANSAS

MICHIGAN

MINNESOTA

MISSOURI

NEBRASKA

NORTH DAKOTA

OHIO

SOUTH DAKOTA

WISCONSIN

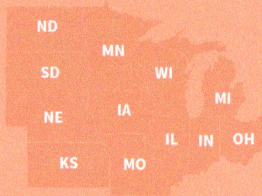

SCHOOL OF THE ART INSTITUTE OF CHICAGO (SAIC)

Address: 36 S. Wabash Ave., Chicago, IL 60603
Website: *https://www.saic.edu/academics/departments/ceramics*
Contact: *https://www.saic.edu/contact/*
Phone: (312) 629-6101
Email: admiss@saic.edu

COST OF ATTENDANCE:

Tuition & Fees: $53,360 | **Additional Expenses:** $21,200
Total: $74,560

Financial Aid: https://www.saic.edu/financial-aid/

ADDITIONAL INFORMATION:

Available Degree(s)

- BFA Studio, area: Ceramics or Sculpture

Portfolio Requirement

Portfolios are required for incoming students. Submit 10-15 recent works.

Scholarships Offered

SAIC offers Presidential, Distinguished, Honors, Recognition, Incentive, and Enrichment scholarships at varied amounts. These merit scholarships are based on the student's portfolio and application materials. In addition, students who participated in certain art exhibitions or competitions may be eligible for the Competitive Excellence Award ($2000).

Need-based scholarships are also available. Some of these include the John and Mary E. Hoggins Scholarship for female SAIC students, the Roger Brown and George Veronda Scholarship, or the LeRoy Neiman Scholarship. Award amounts vary.

Special Opportunities

Studies at SAIC are interdisciplinary, where students do not declare a major and instead freely study among various areas of study. Students at SAIC have access to the internationally-recognized collection of the Art Institute of Chicago. This collection contains a body of work spanning 5,000 years from global artists. Students also have access to large, well-lit classrooms and studios to engage in open discussions and dialogue with faculty and classmates.

Notable Alumni

Samantha Bittman, Anko Chang, Jaye TC Cho, Laura Collins, Alice Cook, Jessica DuPreez, Colin Fleck, Weiyang Gao, Mary Griffin, Patrick Dean Hubbell, Tony Lewis, Kelly Lloyd, Kristy Luck, Ajmal 'Mas Man' Millar, Claire Moore, Aliza Nisenbaum, Ingrid Olson, Angel Otero, Zak Prekop, Celeste Rapone, Alejandro Rojas, Bassim Al Shaker, Margaux Siegel, Jeni Spota, Matthew Sprung, Adrienne Tarver, Alice Tippit, Orkideh Torabi, Maxwell Volkman, and Molly Zuckerman-Hartung

UNIVERSITY OF ILLINOIS URBANA-CHAMPAIGN (UIUC)

Address: 901 West Illinois Street, Urbana, IL 61801
Website: *https://art.illinois.edu/programs-and-applying/bachelors-programs/studio-art-ba-bfa/sculpture/*
Contact: *https://admissions.illinois.edu/contact*
Phone: (217) 333-0302
Email: admissions@illinois.edu

COST OF ATTENDANCE:

In-State Tuition & Fees: $16,866 | **Additional Expenses:** $16,194
Total: $33,060

Out-of-State Tuition & Fees: $34,316 | **Additional Expenses:** $16,534
Total: $50,850

Financial Aid: https://admissions.illinois.edu/Invest/financial-aid

ADDITIONAL INFORMATION:

Available Degree(s)

- BA Studio Art, concentration: Sculpture
- BFA Studio Art, concentration: Sculpture

Portfolio Requirement

Portfolios are required for incoming students. Submit 10 recent works.

Scholarships Offered

Both in-state and out-of-state applicants are eligible for various merit-based and need-based scholarships.

Special Opportunities

At UIUC, students focus on methods related to three-dimensional art, form-making, and expanded spatial practices. Students may utilize equipment in the well-equipped wood-shops, plaster and casting rooms, welding and cold metal fabrication, sewing and fiber studios, 3D printers, vacuum forming machines, digital imaging, and more.

Notable Alumni

Mark Staff Brandl, Christopher Brown, Annie Crawley, Greg Drasler, Leslie Erganian, Hart D. Fisher, Tom Goldenberg, David Klamen, Susan Rankaitis, Angela M. Rivers, Leo Segedin, Deb Sokolow, Lorado Taft, Charles H. Traub, Vivian Zapata, and Barbara Zeigler

ILLINOIS

INDIANA

IOWA

KANSAS

MICHIGAN

MINNESOTA

MISSOURI

NEBRASKA

NORTH DAKOTA

OHIO

SOUTH DAKOTA

WISCONSIN

MIDWEST

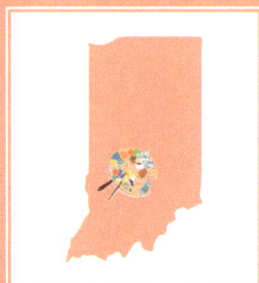

ILLINOIS

INDIANA

IOWA

KANSAS

MICHIGAN

MINNESOTA

MISSOURI

NEBRASKA

NORTH DAKOTA

OHIO

SOUTH DAKOTA

WISCONSIN

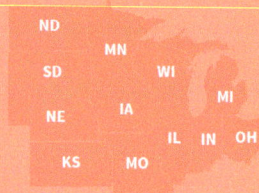

INDIANA UNIVERSITY BLOOMINGTON

Address: 107 S. Indiana Avenue, Bloomington, IN 47405
Website: *https://eskenazi.indiana.edu/undergraduate/majors/studio-bfa.html*
Contact: *https://admissions.indiana.edu/contact/index.html*
Phone: (812) 855-4848
Email: admissions@indiana.edu

COST OF ATTENDANCE:

In-State Tuition & Fees: $11,332 | **Additional Expenses:** $15,966
Total: $27,298

Out-of-State Tuition & Fees: $38,352 | **Additional Expenses:** $15,966
Total: $54,318

Financial Aid: https://admissions.indiana.edu/cost-financial-aid/financial-aid.html

ADDITIONAL INFORMATION:

Available Degree(s)

- BFA Studio Art, concentration: Ceramics, Metals + Jewelry, Sculpture

Portfolio Requirement

Portfolios are not required for incoming students. However, students must undergo a portfolio review at some point during their undergraduate studies in order to be accepted into the BFA program.

Scholarships Offered

Indiana University Bloomington offers a variety of scholarships for in-state, out-of-state, and international students. Students applying before the early action deadline will receive consideration for IU Academic Scholarships ($1,000–$11,000) and for the invitation-only Selective Scholarship.

Special Opportunities

Students may be interested in studying abroad. Popular programs for studio art majors include studying in Italy, Guatemala, Japan, and Barcelona. In the studio art program, students take coursework such as Digital Art, Printmaking Media, Video Art, Anatomy for the Artist, and more.

Notable Alumni

Lyndall Bass, Tim Downs, Lissa Hunter, and Komelia Hongja Okim

UNIVERSITY OF KANSAS

Address: 1502 Iowa St., Lawrence, KS 66045
Website: *https://art.ku.edu/degrees*
Contact: *https://admissions.ku.edu/reps*
Phone: (785) 864-3911
Email: adm@ku.edu

COST OF ATTENDANCE:

In-State Tuition & Fees: $ | **Additional Expenses:** $
Total: $

Out-of-State Tuition & Fees: $ | **Additional Expenses:** $
Total: $

Financial Aid: https://financialaid.ku.edu/

ADDITIONAL INFORMATION:

Available Degree(s)

- BFA Ceramics
- BFA Metalsmithing/Jewelry
- BFA Visual Art
- BA Visual Art

Portfolio Requirement

Portfolios are required for incoming students.

Scholarships Offered

University of Kansas offers various merit-based and need-based schoalrships to incoming students. In-state students may qualify for up to $20,000 across four years, while out-of-state students may earn up to $64,000 in aid across four years.

Special Opportunities

In the visual art program, students spend their first year developing foundational technical skills and expanding their creativity. In the second year, students choose coursework across the seven studio areas. This interdisciplinary approach allows students to learn across various artistic mediums in order to make an informed decision about their chosen area of study in the third and fourth year.

Notable Alumni

Gina Adams, Ann Hamilton, Jack Lembeck, Heidi Schwegler, Gary Mark Smith, and Robert Morris

ILLINOIS

INDIANA

IOWA

KANSAS

MICHIGAN

MINNESOTA

MISSOURI

NEBRASKA

NORTH DAKOTA

OHIO

SOUTH DAKOTA

WISCONSIN

MIDWEST

ILLINOIS

INDIANA

IOWA

KANSAS

MICHIGAN

MINNESOTA

MISSOURI

NEBRASKA

NORTH DAKOTA

OHIO

SOUTH DAKOTA

WISCONSIN

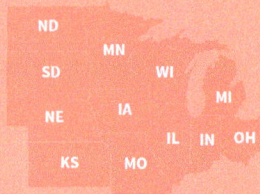

COLLEGE FOR CREATIVE STUDIES

Address: 201 E. Kirby, Detroit, MI 48202
Website: *https://www.collegeforcreativestudies.edu/academics/undergraduate-programs/crafts/*
Contact: *https://www.collegeforcreativestudies.edu/contact-us*
Phone: (313) 664-7425
Email: admissions@collegeforcreativestudies.edu

COST OF ATTENDANCE:

Tuition & Fees: $48,030 | **Additional Expenses:** $10,577
Total: $58,607

Financial Aid: https://www.collegeforcreativestudies.edu/admissions/scholarship-aid

ADDITIONAL INFORMATION:

Available Degree(s)

- BFA Craft and Material Studies

Portfolio Requirement

Portfolios are required for incoming students. Submit at least 8 pieces of work completed within the past two years. Submit via SlideRoom.

Scholarships Offered

Applicants are automatically considered for CCS scholarships. CCS encourages students to explore outside scholarship opportunities.

Special Opportunities

There are five specialities that students may explore within the major: Ceramics, Fiber & Textiles, Glass, Metalsmithing & Jewelry, or Digital Fabrication. Students in the program learn foundational technical skills as well as business entrepreneurship. All students are encouraged to pursue internship opportunities as undergraduates.

Notable Alumni

Kevin Beasley, Harry Bertoia, Doug Chiang, Wendy Froud, and Renée Radell

UNIVERSITY OF MICHIGAN

Address: 500 S. State St., Ann Arbor, MI 48109
Website: *https://stamps.umich.edu/undergraduate-programs/bfa*
Contact: *https://umich.edu/contact/*
Phone: (734) 764-7433
Email: https://admissions.umich.edu/explore-visit/contact-us

COST OF ATTENDANCE:

In-State Tuition & Fees: $15,558 | **Additional Expenses:** $15,498
Total: $31,056

Out-of-State Tuition & Fees: $51,200 | **Additional Expenses:** $15,498
Total: $66,698

Financial Aid: https://finaid.umich.edu/

ADDITIONAL INFORMATION:

Available Degree(s)

- BFA Art & Design

Portfolio Requirement

Portfolios are required for incoming students. Submit 12-15 works, 2 of which are direct observaitonal drawings. Submit via SlideRoom.

Scholarships Offered

University of Michigan offers several scholarships for incoming students. One of them is the Stamps Scholars Program, a prestigious merit-based program that offers the full cost of attendance. The HAIL Scholarship is an invitational award that covers four years of tuition and fees for low-income, high achieving Michigan students. Many scholarships are need-based, although some are merit-based as well.

Special Opportunities

As with most BFA Art programs, University of Michigan requires a sophomore review where students present their work in front of a faculty panel. A successful sophomore review is required for continuation in the program. The International Experience is a unique opportunity for Stamps graduates to enter the international arena for fellowship opportunities and employment. Students are required to attend an approved study abroad institution during their undergraduate studies.

Notable Alumni

Benny Alba, Bill Barrett, Michele Oka Doner, Mike Kelley, Robert Nickle, Jason Polan, Alison Ruttan, Eric Staller, and Bernard "Tony" Rosenthal

ILLINOIS

INDIANA

IOWA

KANSAS

MICHIGAN

MINNESOTA

MISSOURI

NEBRASKA

NORTH DAKOTA

OHIO

SOUTH DAKOTA

WISCONSIN

MIDWEST

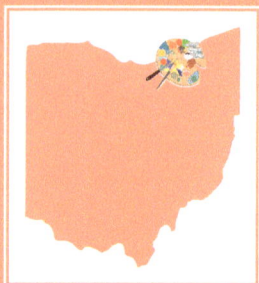

ILLINOIS

INDIANA

IOWA

KANSAS

MICHIGAN

MINNESOTA

MISSOURI

NEBRASKA

NORTH DAKOTA

OHIO

SOUTH DAKOTA

WISCONSIN

CLEVELAND INSTITUTE OF ART

Address: 11610 Euclid Avenue, Cleveland, OH 44106
Website: *https://www.cia.edu/academics/majors*
Contact: *https://www.cia.edu/contact*
Phone: (216) 421-7000
Email: admissions@cia.edu

COST OF ATTENDANCE:

Tuition & Fees: $45,495 | **Additional Expenses:** $17,010
Total: $62,505

Financial Aid: https://www.cia.edu/admissions/financing-your-education

ADDITIONAL INFORMATION:

Available Degree(s)

- BFA Craft & Design
- BFA Sculpture & Expanded Media

Portfolio Requirement

Portfolios are required for incoming students. Submit 12-20 works via SlideRoom. Sketchbook pages are highly encouraged. Do not include works copied from photographs.

Scholarships Offered

CIA offers renewable merit scholarships to undergraduate students. Students are automatically considered upon acceptance. Students who do not receive a merit scholarship may still be considered for a need-based CIA grant if they submit a FAFSA.

Special Opportunities

CIA's Engage Practice is a feature of the school that provides students with the opportunity to work on real-world projects with external clients while they complete their studies. Students gain professional experience that will help them tremendously post-graduation. Sculpture students learn construction skills, woodworking, textile and metal fabrication, 3D modeling, casting, sewing, sound manipulation, and more.

Notable Alumni

Richard Anuszkiewicz, Samuel Bookatz, Leigh Brooklyn, Martha Elizabeth Burchfield Richter, Ray Burggraf, Rosana Castrillo Diaz, Shan Goshorn, Sante Graziani, Leamon Green, Mark Greenwold, Marsden Hartley, Bob Paul Kane, Victor Kord, Betty LaDuke, Robert Munford, Gertrude L. Pew, Glenora Richards, Jason Schoener, Jenny Scobel, Brain Shure, Judy Takács, Ann Toebbe, Frank N. Wilcox, Thaddeus Wolfe, and Harold Zisla

COLUMBUS COLLEGE OF ART AND DESIGN

Address: 60 Cleveland Ave, Columbus, OH 43215
Website: *https://www.ccad.edu/academics/fine-arts*
Contact: *https://www.ccad.edu/directory*
Phone: (614) 224-9101
Email: admissions@ccad.edu

COST OF ATTENDANCE:

Tuition & Fees: $37,370 | **Additional Expenses:** $17,208
Total: $54,578

Financial Aid: https://www.ccad.edu/admissions/financial-aid

ADDITIONAL INFORMATION:

Available Degree(s)

- BFA Fine Arts, concentrations: Ceramics, Glass, Jewelry, or Sculpture

Portfolio Requirement

Portfolios are required for incoming students. Submit 8-15 pieces of work.

Scholarships Offered

CCAD offers academic and merit scholarships. There are also external scholarship opportunities, such as the Ohio Governor's Youth Art Exhibition, the Lounge Lizard scholarship competition, MVP Scholarships ($500) and more.

Special Opportunities

Students in the fine arts program take intensive studio coursework and expand their technical skills in a variety of areas, such as drawing, printmaking, ceramics, jewelry, sculpture, and glass. Facilities include two student galleries, a sculpture lab, a woodshop, welding lab, foundry, ceramics studio, printmaking lab, glass studio, jewelry studio, and a tool room with state-of-the-art equipment.

Notable Alumni

Ming Fay, Jerry McDaniel, Aminah Robinson, and Choi Yan-chi

ILLINOIS

INDIANA

IOWA

KANSAS

MICHIGAN

MINNESOTA

MISSOURI

NEBRASKA

NORTH DAKOTA

OHIO

SOUTH DAKOTA

WISCONSIN

MIDWEST

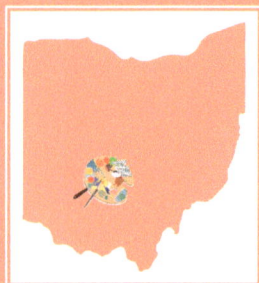

ILLINOIS

INDIANA

IOWA

KANSAS

MICHIGAN

MINNESOTA

MISSOURI

NEBRASKA

NORTH DAKOTA

OHIO

SOUTH DAKOTA

WISCONSIN

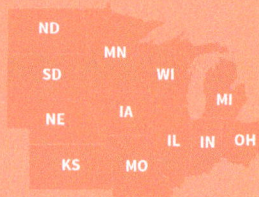

THE OHIO STATE UNIVERSITY

Address: 1849 Cannon Drive, Columbus, OH 43210
Website: *https://art.osu.edu/undergraduate-studies*
Contact: *http://undergrad.osu.edu/contact-us*
Phone: (614) 292-5821
Email: askabuckeye@osu.edu

COST OF ATTENDANCE:

In-State Tuition & Fees: $11,518 | **Additional Expenses:** $17,146
Total: $28,664

Out-of-State Tuition & Fees: $33,502 | **Additional Expenses:** $17,980
Total: $51,482

Financial Aid: https://sfa.osu.edu/

ADDITIONAL INFORMATION:

Available Degree(s)

- BFA Art, emphases: Ceramics, Glass, or Sculpture

Portfolio Requirement

Portfolios are not required for incoming students. However, undergraduate students must later apply to their area of emphasis during their studies.

Scholarships Offered

University merit scholarships include the Eminence Fellows Program and Scholarship (full cost of attendance for 8 semesters), the Morrill Scholarship Program, the Maximus Scholarship ($3,000 per year), and several others.

Special Opportunities

Students must take a core sequence of courses for their first two years of study. In their second year, students prepare their portfolios for acceptance into an area of emphasis. OSU offers a minor in Art: Engineering Structure that integrates artistic studio practice with research pursuits. The minor focuses on material exploration and helps students develop process-based skills.

Notable Alumni

Charles Csuri, Rick Mills, Joseph W. Papin, Christopher Ries, and Graeme Sullivan

UNIVERSITY OF WISCONSIN, MADISON

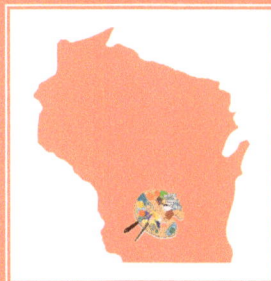

Address: 702 West Johnson Street, Madison, WI 53715
Website: *https://art.wisc.edu/media-disciplines/3d/*
Contact: *https://admissions.wisc.edu/contact-us/*
Phone: (608) 262-3961
Email: onwisconsin@admissions.wisc.edu

COST OF ATTENDANCE:

In-State Tuition & Fees: $10,766 | **Additional Expenses:** $16,764
Total: $27,530

Out-of-State Tuition & Fees: $38,654 | **Additional Expenses:** $17,234
Total: $55,888

MN Resident Tuition & Fees: $14,812 | **Additional Expenses:** $17,044
Total: $31,856

Financial Aid: https://financialaid.wisc.edu/

ADDITIONAL INFORMATION:

Available Degree(s)

- BFA Art, concentration: Contemporary 3D Practices

Portfolio Requirement

Portfolios are not required for incoming students, however they are strongly recommended. Applicants must submit a portfolio to be considered for the incoming art scholarships.

Scholarships Offered

The University of Wisconsin offers various institutional awards. Students may apply through the Wisconsin Scholarship Hub (WiSH).

Special Opportunities

In Contemporary 3D Practices, students learn techniques in ceramics, glass, neon, art metals, jewelry, sculpture, woodworking, and furniture design. UW Madison houses the first collegiate Glass program in the nation, founded in 1962. It is considered by many to be the birthplace of American studio glass. Furthermore, UW Madison is one of five universities in the country with a program in neon.

Notable Alumni

Gary Beecham, Kate Borcherding, Dale Chihuly, Hunter Cole, Joe Feddersen, Honor Ford-Smith, MK Guth, Sam Herman, Marvin Lipofsky, Bruce Nauman, Jennifer Nehrbass, Jon Schueler, Michael Velliquette, and Nancy Metz White

ILLINOIS

INDIANA

IOWA

KANSAS

MICHIGAN

MINNESOTA

MISSOURI

NEBRASKA

NORTH DAKOTA

OHIO

SOUTH DAKOTA

WISCONSIN

MIDWEST

ALABAMA

ARKANSAS

DELAWARE

DISTRICT OF
COLUMBIA

FLORIDA

GEORGIA

KENTUCKY

LOUISIANA

MARYLAND

MISSISSIPPI

NORTH CAROLINA

OKLAHOMA

SOUTH CAROLINA

TENNESSEE

TEXAS

VIRGINIA

WEST VIRGINIA

CHAPTER 14

REGION THREE

SOUTH

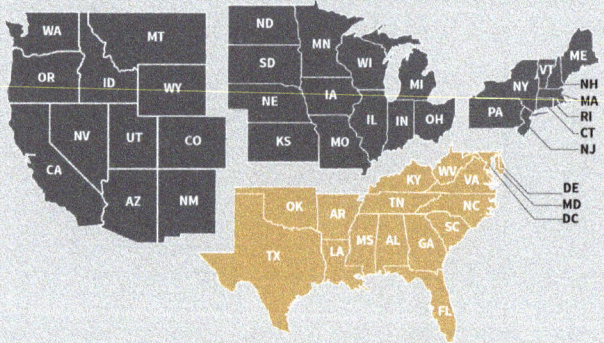

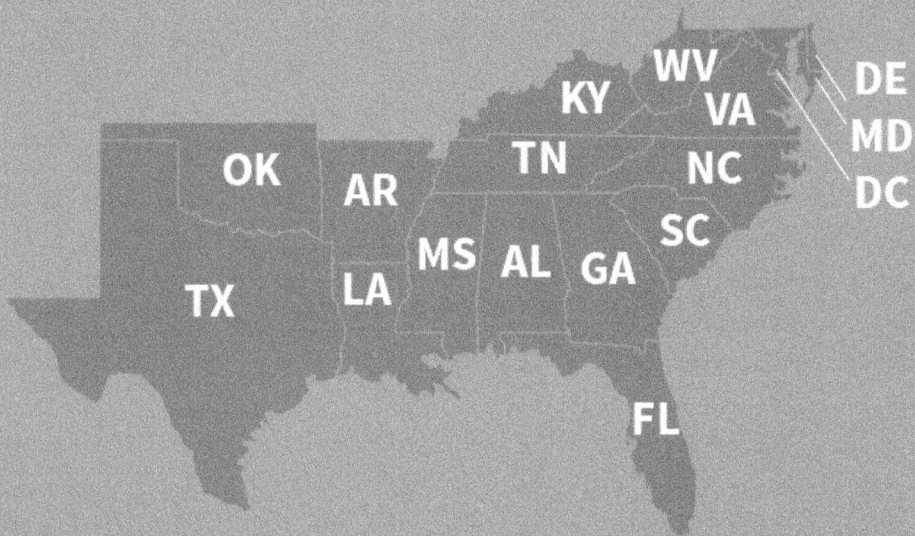

6 *Programs* | 16 *States*

1. FL – Ringling College of Art and Design
2. GA - Savannah College of Art and Design (SCAD)
3. GA - University of Georgia
4. MD - Maryland Institute College of Art
5. TX - University of North Texas
6. VA - Virginia Commonwealth University

3D ART & DESIGN PROGRAMS

School	Avg. GPA, SAT Evidence-Based Reading Writing (ERW), SAT Math (M), and ACT Composite (C) — Early Decision (ED): Yes/No	Admission Statistics	Program(s)	Portfolio Required (req.)
Ringling College of Art & Design 2700 N. Tamiami Trail, Sarasota, FL 34234	GPA: N/A SAT (ERW): N/A* SAT (M): N/A* ACT (C): N/A* *Test-optional ED: No	Overall College Admit Rate: 69% Undergrad Enrollment: 1,624 Total Enrollment: 1,624	BFA Fine Arts	Portfolio req.
Savannah College of Art & Design (SCAD) 342 Bull St., Savannah, GA 31401	GPA: 3.6 SAT (ERW): 540-640 SAT (M): 500-600 ACT (C): 20-27 ED: No	Admit Rate: 78% Undergrad Enrollment: 11,679 Total Enrollment: 14,265	BFA Accessory Design BFA Jewelry BFA Sculpture	Portfolio req.
University of Georgia Dawson Hall, 305 Sanford Dr., Athens, GA 30602	GPA: 4.02 SAT (ERW): 620-700 SAT (M): 600-720 ACT (C): ED: No	Admit Rate: 48% Undergrad Enrollment: 29,765 Total Enrollment: 39,147	BFA Art, concentrations: Ceramics Jewelry & Metalwork Sculpture	Portfolio not req.
Maryland Institute College of Art (MICA) 1300 W. Mount Royal Ave., Baltimore, MD 21217	GPA: N/A SAT (ERW): N/A SAT (M): N/A ACT (C): N/A *Test-optional ED: Yes	Admit Rate: 90% Undergrad Enrollment: 1,331 Total Enrollment: 1,892	BFA Ceramics BFA Interdisciplinary Sculpture	Portfolio req.

School	Avg. GPA, SAT Evidence-Based Reading Writing (ERW), SAT Math (M), and ACT Composite (C) Early Decision (ED): Yes/No	Admission Statistics	Program(s)	Portfolio Required (req.)
University of North Texas Chilton Hall 331, 410 S. Avenue C, Denton, TX 76201	GPA: N/A SAT (ERW): 530-630 SAT (M): 520-610 ACT (C): ED: No	Admit Rate: 84% Undergrad Enrollment: 32,814 Total Enrollment: 40,953	BFA Studio Art, concentrations: Ceramics Metalsmithing & Jewelry Sculpture	Portfolio req.
Virginia Commonwealth University Virginia Commonwealth University, Richmond, VA 23284	GPA: 3.72 SAT (ERW): 540-640 SAT (M): 520-610 ACT (C): 21-28 ED: No	Admit Rate: 91% Undergrad Enrollment: 21,943 Total Enrollment: 29,070	BFA Craft and Material Studies BFA Sculpture	Portfolio req.

SOUTH

ALABAMA

ARKANSAS

DELAWARE

DISTRICT OF
COLUMBIA

FLORIDA

GEORGIA

KENTUCKY

LOUISIANA

MARYLAND

MISSISSIPPI

NORTH CAROLINA

OKLAHOMA

SOUTH CAROLINA

TENNESSEE

TEXAS

VIRGINIA

WEST VIRGINIA

RINGLING COLLEGE OF ART & DESIGN

Address: 2700 N. Tamiami Trail, Sarasota, FL 34234
Website: *https://www.ringling.edu/fine-arts/*
Contact: *https://www.ringling.edu/contact*
Phone: (941) 351–5100
Email: admissions@ringling.edu

COST OF ATTENDANCE:

Tuition & Fees: $49,649 | **Additional Expenses:** $22,025
Total: $71,674

Financial Aid: https://www.ringling.edu/financialaid

ADDITIONAL INFORMATION:

Available Degree(s)

- BFA Fine Arts

Portfolio Requirement

Portfolios are required for incoming students. Submit via SlideRoom. Applicants must include drawings from observation. Copying other artists is not permitted. Applicants must also avoid cliches, such as anime, tattoos, dragons, or unicorns.

Scholarships Offered

Ringling College offers merit scholarships and need-based grants. Some of the scholarships include the Presidential Scholarship ($25,000 per year for 4 years), the Dean's Scholarship ($10,000 per year for 4 years), the Faculty Scholarship ($8,000 per year for 4 years) and several others.

Special Opportunities

Students in the Fine Arts program build upon their critical thinking, painting, drawing, sculpture, printmaking, and technology skills. They are given designated studio spaces and have access to facilities and exhibition opportunities in Ringling's Studios North facility. This area is exclusive to Fine Arts students.

Notable Alumni

Melvin Gomez, Tim Jaeger, Andrew Jones, Tim Rogerson, and Mike Zeck

SAVANNAH COLLEGE OF ART & DESIGN (SCAD)

Address: 342 Bull St., Savannah, GA 31401
Website: *https://www.scad.edu/academics/programs?location=all&program=undergraduate&school=all*
Contact: *https://www.scad.edu/about/contact*
Phone: (912) 525-5100
Email: contact@scad.edu
Other locations: Atlanta, GA

COST OF ATTENDANCE:

Tuition & Fees: $38,340 | **Additional Expenses:** $15,269
Total: $53,609

Financial Aid: https://www.scad.edu/admission/financial-aid-and-scholarships

ADDITIONAL INFORMATION:

Available Degree(s)

- BFA Accessory Design
- BFA Jewelry
- BFA Sculpture

Portfolio Requirement

Portfolios are required for incoming students. Applicants may choose any of the following categories, whether or not it reflects their intended major: Business & Marketing, Visual Art, Time-Based Media, Writing, Equestrian, or Performing Arts. However, SCAD suggests applicants should curate a portfolio that demonstrates the applicant's interests and aptitude. Submit via SlideRoom.

Scholarships Offered

All applicants including international students are eligible for merit-scholarships. The May and Paul Poetter Scholarship awards full tuition and is based on academic achievement. The Frances Larkin McCommon Scholarship awards full tuition and is based on artistic achievement. SCAD also offers SCAD academic scholarships ($1,500-$12,000). Among grants, the SCAD Athletic Grant awards $2,000-$12,000. Furthermore, students may receive a scholarship award via the SCAD Challenge Scholarship. Awards range from $2,000-$4,000.

Special Opportunities

At SCAD, students engage in technical skill-building while also networking with students and alumni. Minors that complement the program include ceramic arts, sculpture, printmaking, photography, and jewelry. Students may take coursework in The Design of Business, Rapid Prototyping, Light, Sound, & the Projected Image, Rendering for Jewelry Design, and more.

Notable Alumni

Jill Bullitt, Luna Brothers, M. Alice LeGrow, and Meredith Pardue

ALABAMA
ARKANSAS
DELAWARE
DISTRICT OF COLUMBIA
FLORIDA
GEORGIA
KENTUCKY
LOUISIANA
MARYLAND
MISSISSIPPI
NORTH CAROLINA
OKLAHOMA
SOUTH CAROLINA
TENNESSEE
TEXAS
VIRGINIA
WEST VIRGINIA

SOUTH

ALABAMA

ARKANSAS

DELAWARE

DISTRICT OF
COLUMBIA

FLORIDA

GEORGIA

KENTUCKY

LOUISIANA

MARYLAND

MISSISSIPPI

NORTH CAROLINA

OKLAHOMA

SOUTH CAROLINA

TENNESSEE

TEXAS

VIRGINIA

WEST VIRGINIA

UNIVERSITY OF GEORGIA

Address: Lamar Dodd School of Art, 270 River Road, Athens, GA 30602
Website: *https://art.uga.edu/academics/undergraduate-studies*
Contact: *https://reg.uga.edu/general-information/contact-us/*
Phone: (706) 542-1511
Email: undergrad@admissions.uga.edu

COST OF ATTENDANCE:

In-State Tuition & Fees: $12,068 | **Additional Expenses:** $15,878
Total: $27,946

Out-of-State Tuition & Fees: $31,108 | **Additional Expenses:** $16,252
Total: $47,360

Financial Aid: https://osfa.uga.edu/

ADDITIONAL INFORMATION:

Available Degree(s)

- BFA Art, concentrations: Ceramics, Jewelry & Metalwork, or Sculpture

Portfolio Requirement

Portfolios are not required for incoming students. However, students must undergo a portfolio review at the end of their second year.

Scholarships Offered

The University of Georgia offers numerous academic-based, need-based, and both academic and need-based aids to students, many of which are open to Georgia residents, out-of-state students, and international students. Awards go as high as $22,900.

Special Opportunities

The BFA in Art requires the Studio Art Core, a year-long dive into art history, studio foundations, methodologies, and upper-level coursework in interdisciplinary studio work and professional practices. After the second year of study, students apply to their area of concentration. A capstone project is required prior to graduation.

Notable Alumni

Jack Davis, Tom Deitz, Leonard DeLonga, Scott Hill, and Sarah Hobbs

MARYLAND INSTITUTE COLLEGE OF ART (MICA)

Address: 1300 W. Mount Royal Ave., Baltimore, MD 21217
Website: *https://www.mica.edu/undergraduate-majors-minors/*
Contact: *https://www.mica.edu/mica-dna/contact-us/*
Phone: (410) 669-9200
Email: https://www.mica.edu/forms/contact-undergraduate-admission/

COST OF ATTENDANCE:

Tuition & Fees: $53,333 | **Additional Expenses:** $17,820
Total: $71,153

Financial Aid: https://www.mica.edu/financial-aid/

ADDITIONAL INFORMATION:

Available Degree(s)

- BFA Ceramics
- BFA Interdisciplinary Sculpture

Portfolio Requirement

Portfolios are required for incoming students. Submit 12-20 works. MICA strongly suggests including drawings from observation rather than from imagination or copied from photographs.

Scholarships Offered

MICA offers several, competitive merit-based scholarships to all incoming undergraduate students. Some of these offers include the Mathias J. Devito Scholarship Program ($40,000 over 4 years), the Fanny B. Thalheimer Scholarship ($16,000-$68,000 over four years), the Academic Excellence Scholarships ($12,000-$24,000) and several others.

Special Opportunities

Students learn techniques in woodworking, metal fabrication, mold-making, casting, laser cutting, 3D prototyping, welding, carving, assembling, and more. Students are encouraged to develop technical mastery along with a conceptual understanding of emerging genres.

Notable Alumni

Nina Akamu, Matt Johnson, Ernest Keyser, Jeff Koons, Gwen Lux, James Earl Reid, William Henry Rinehart, Jacolby Satterwhite, Hans Schuler, Joyce J. Scott, and Jen Stark

ALABAMA
ARKANSAS
DELAWARE
DISTRICT OF COLUMBIA
FLORIDA
GEORGIA
KENTUCKY
LOUISIANA
MARYLAND
MISSISSIPPI
NORTH CAROLINA
OKLAHOMA
SOUTH CAROLINA
TENNESSEE
TEXAS
VIRGINIA
WEST VIRGINIA

SOUTH

ALABAMA

ARKANSAS

DELAWARE

DISTRICT OF COLUMBIA

FLORIDA

GEORGIA

KENTUCKY

LOUISIANA

MARYLAND

MISSISSIPPI

NORTH CAROLINA

OKLAHOMA

SOUTH CAROLINA

TENNESSEE

TEXAS

VIRGINIA

WEST VIRGINIA

UNIVERSITY OF NORTH TEXAS

Address: 1201 W. Mulberry St., Denton, TX 76201
Website: *https://cvad.unt.edu/studioart#bfa*
Contact: *https://admissions.unt.edu/contact-us*
Phone: (940) 565-2855
Email: undergrad@unt.edu

COST OF ATTENDANCE:

In-State Tuition & Fees: $11,514 | **Additional Expenses:** $13,860
Total: $25,374

Out-of-State Tuition & Fees: $24,514 | **Additional Expenses:** $13,860
Total: $38,374

Financial Aid: https://financialaid.unt.edu/

ADDITIONAL INFORMATION:

Available Degree(s)

- BFA Studio Art, concentrations: Ceramics, Metalsmithing & Jewelry, or Sculpture

Portfolio Requirement

Portfolios are required for incoming students. Submit 12 works in various media. Ensure that 2-12 of your pieces are observational. An artist statement is also required.

Scholarships Offered

Merit-based awards offered at University of North Texas include the UNT Excellence Scholarship ($1,000-$12,000) and the UNT Meritorious Scholarship for National Merit Finalists (full cost of attendance). Out-of-state and international students who receive UNT Excellence Scholarship are eligible for a Texas state competitive scholarship waiver for the difference between in-state and out-of-state tuition.

Special Opportunities

In the Studio Art program, students prepare for a career in the arts by expanding their technical skills, engaging in team-based learning, and participating in critical analysis.

Notable Alumni

Elliot Johnson, Michael Lark, Elizabeth McDonald, and Xiaoze Xie

VIRGINIA COMMONWEALTH UNIVERSITY

Address: Virginia Commonwealth University, Richmond, VA 23284
Website: *https://arts.vcu.edu/academics/departments/craft-material-studies/*
Contact: *https://www.vcu.edu/contacts/*
Phone: (804) 828-0100
Email: ugrad@vcu.edu

COST OF ATTENDANCE:

In-State Tuition & Fees: $17,140 | **Additional Expenses:** $17,549
Total: $34,689

Out-of-State Tuition & Fees: $38,478 | **Additional Expenses:** $17,549
Total: $56,027

Financial Aid: https://finaid.vcu.edu/

ADDITIONAL INFORMATION:

Available Degree(s)

- BFA Craft and Material Studies
- BFA Sculpture

Portfolio Requirement

Portfolios are required for incoming students. Submit 12-16 works created over the past two years. Applicants are encouraged to include drawings from observation and discouraged to include copied work.

Scholarships Offered

First-year students may be eligible for VCUarts talent scholarships ($5,000-$12,000 annually) if they apply by January 15th. Students are automatically considered and eligibility is based on academic merit and artistic talent. In addition, all students are automatically considered for institutional scholarships if they apply by November 15th. University scholarship awards vary based on the scholarship, but range from $8,000 per year to $16,000 plus room and board per year.

Special Opportunities

Students at VCU frequently travel and learn more about artistic influence in various communities. Visits to galleries, museums, and studios across the country and the world are encouraged. All students are also encouraged to participate in the annual program to Peru each summer.

Notable Alumni

Diana al-Hadid, Trudy Benson, Tara Donovan, Lisa Hoke, Nate Lewis, Whitney Lynn, Eric Millikin, and Carol Sutton

ALABAMA
ARKANSAS
DELAWARE
DISTRICT OF COLUMBIA
FLORIDA
GEORGIA
KENTUCKY
LOUISIANA
MARYLAND
MISSISSIPPI
NORTH CAROLINA
OKLAHOMA
SOUTH CAROLINA
TENNESSEE
TEXAS
VIRGINIA
WEST VIRGINIA

SOUTH

ALASKA

ARIZONA

CALIFORNIA

COLORADO

HAWAII

IDAHO

MONTANA

NEVADA

NEW MEXICO

OREGON

UTAH

WASHINGTON

WYOMING

CHAPTER 15

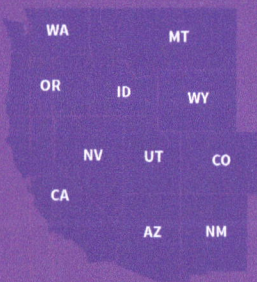

CHAPTER 15
REGION FOUR
WEST

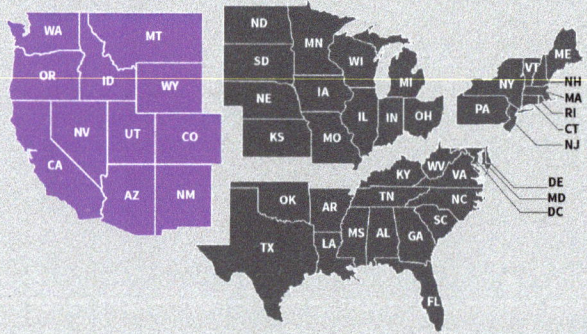

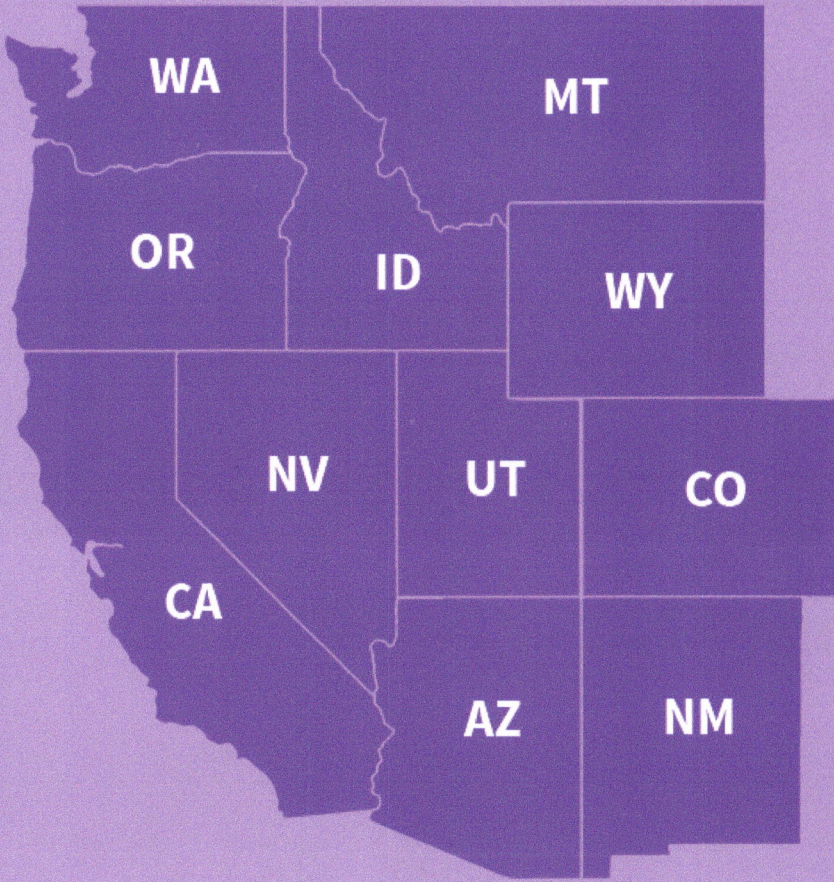

8 *Programs* | **13** *States*

1. *CA - Academy of Art University*
2. *CA - California College of the Arts (CCA)*
3. *CA - California Institute of the Arts (CalArts)*
4. *CA - Laguna College of Art and Design*
5. *CA - University of California, Los Angeles (UCLA)*
6. *OR - University of Oregon*
7. *WA - Central Washington University*
8. *WA - University of Washington*

School	Avg. GPA, SAT Evidence-Based Reading Writing (ERW), SAT Math (M), and ACT Composite (C) Early Decision (ED): Yes/No	Admission Statistics	Program(s)	Portfolio Required (req.)
Academy of Art University 79 New Montgomery St., San Francisco, CA 94105	GPA: N/A SAT (ERW): N/A SAT (M): N/A ACT (C): N/A *Academy of Art has an open admissions policy. ED: No	Admit Rate: N/A Undergrad Enrollment: 6,124 Total Enrollment: 8,928	BFA Fine Art, emphasis: Sculpture	Portfolio not req.
California College of the Arts (CCA) 1111 Eighth St., San Francisco, CA 94107	GPA: N/A SAT (ERW): N/A* SAT (M): N/A* ACT (C): N/A* *Test-optional ED: No	Overall College Admit Rate: 85% Undergrad Enrollment: 1,239 Total Enrollment: 1,612	BFA Ceramics BFA Glass BFA Jewelry & Metal Arts BFA Sculpture	Portfolio req.
California Institute of the Arts (CalArts) 24700 McBean Pkwy., Valencia, CA 91355	GPA: N/A SAT (ERW): N/A* SAT (M): N/A* ACT (C): N/A* *Test-optional ED: Yes	Overall College Admit Rate: 32% Undergrad Enrollment: 783 Total Enrollment: 1,189	BFA Art	Portfolio req.
Laguna College of Art and Design 2222 Laguna Canyon Rd., Laguna Beach, CA 92651	GPA: N/A SAT (ERW): 710-760 SAT (M): 770-800 ACT (C): 34-36 ED: No	Admit Rate: 83% Undergrad Enrollment: 732 Total Enrollment: 782	BFA Drawing + Painting, emphasis: Sculpture	Portfolio req.

School	Avg. GPA, SAT Evidence-Based Reading Writing (ERW), SAT Math (M), and ACT Composite (C) **Early Decision (ED): Yes/No**	Admission Statistics	Program(s)	Portfolio Required (req.)
University of California, Los Angeles (UCLA) 405 Hilgard Avenue, Los Angeles, CA 90095	GPA: 3.9 SAT (ERW): 650-740 SAT (M): 640-780 ACT (C): 29-34 ED: No	Overall College Admit Rate: 14% Undergrad Enrollment: 31,636 Total Enrollment: 44,589	BA Art, concentrations: Ceramics Sculpture	Portfolio req.
University of Oregon 5249 University of Oregon, Eugene, OR 97403	GPA: 3.65 SAT (ERW): 550-650 SAT (M): 540-640 ACT (C): 22-29 ED: No	Overall College Admit Rate: 84% Undergrad Enrollment: 18,045 Total Enrollment: 21,752	BFA Art, areas: Ceramics Jewelry & Metalsmithing Sculpture BA Art, areas: Ceramics Jewelry & Metalsmithing Sculpture	Portfolio not req.
Central Washington University 400 E University Way, Ellensburg, WA 98926	GPA: 3.09 SAT (ERW): 470-580 SAT (M): 460-570 ACT (C): 17-24 ED: No	Overall College Admit Rate: 86% Undergrad Enrollment: 10,518 Total Enrollment: 11,174	BFA Studio Art	Portfolio req.

WEST

3D ART & DESIGN PROGRAMS

School	Avg. GPA, SAT Evidence-Based Reading Writing (ERW), SAT Math (M), and ACT Composite (C)	Admission Statistics	Program(s)	Portfolio Required (req.)
	Early Decision (ED): Yes/No			
University of Washington 1400 NE Campus Parkway, Seattle, WA, 98195	GPA: 3.82 SAT (ERW): 590-700 SAT (M): 610-753 ACT (C): 27-33 ED: No	Overall College Admit Rate: 56% Undergrad Enrollment: 32,244 Total Enrollment: 48,149	BA Art, concentration: 3D4M: ceramics + glass + sculpture	Portfolio not req.

ALASKA

ARIZONA

CALIFORNIA

COLORADO

HAWAII

IDAHO

MONTANA

NEVADA

NEW MEXICO

OREGON

UTAH

WASHINGTON

WYOMING

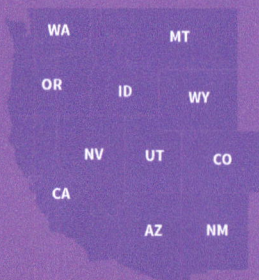

ACADEMY OF ART UNIVERSITY

Address: 79 New Montgomery St., San Francisco, CA 94105
Website: *https://www.academyart.edu/academics/fine-art/*
Contact: *https://my.academyart.edu/directories/admissions*
Phone: (800) 544-2787
Email: admissions@academyart.edu

COST OF ATTENDANCE:

Tuition & Fees: $26,399 | **Additional Expenses:** N/A
Total: $26,399

Financial Aid: https://www.academyart.edu/finances/types-of-financial-aid/

ADDITIONAL INFORMATION:

Available Degree(s)

- BFA Fine Art, emphasis: Sculpture

Portfolio Requirement

Portfolios are not required for incoming students.

Scholarships Offered

The Emerging Artist Scholarship offers awards up to $3,000. International Art & Design Scholarship awards a limited number of scholarships (up to $2,000) to international students.

Special Opportunities

In the sculpture emphasis, students take coursework such as Figure Drawing, Introduction to Anatomy, Still Life Painting, Head & Figure Sculpture, Bronze Casting, Designing Careers, Book Arts, Animal Sculpture, Clothed Figure Drawing, and more. Students are also encouraged to study abroad and take the Painting Study Abroad, Florence Italcy elective.

Notable Alumni

Gema Alava, Corey Arnold, Cheeming Boey, Scott Campbell, Susan Guevara, Laura Ann Jacobs, and Mark Newman

CALIFORNIA COLLEGE OF THE ARTS (CCA)

Address: 1111 Eighth St., San Francisco, CA 94107
Website: https://www.cca.edu/academics/#section-undergraduate
Contact: Contact via phone or email.
Phone: (800) 447-1278
Email: info@cca.edu

COST OF ATTENDANCE:

Tuition & Fees: $54,726 | **Additional Expenses:** $25,255
Total: $79,981

Financial Aid: https://www.cca.edu/admissions/tuition/#section-financial-aid

ADDITIONAL INFORMATION:

Available Degree(s)

- BFA Ceramics
- BFA Glass
- BFA Jewelry & Metal Arts
- BFA Sculpture

Portfolio Requirement

Portfolios are required for incoming students. Submit 10-15 works via SlideRoom.

Scholarships Offered

Merit-based, need-based, CCA-named, and other scholarships available.

Special Opportunities

Rigorous critique and interdisciplinary approaches are at the heart of teaching at CCA. Students build their technical and conceptual skills via intensive studio coursework and engage in dialogue with faculty, peers, and visiting artists. During the third year, students receive their own studio space and then upgrade to a larger space in their last year. This individualized space allows students to complete their thesis projects.

Notable Alumni

Kate Ali, Robert Arneson, Nicole Chesney, Viola Frey, Bryan Nash Gill, Bob Haozous, Dorothy Riber Joralemon, Manuel Neri, Adrien Segal, and Peter Voulkos

ALASKA

ARIZONA

CALIFORNIA

COLORADO

HAWAII

IDAHO

MONTANA

NEVADA

NEW MEXICO

OREGON

UTAH

WASHINGTON

WYOMING

WEST

ALASKA

ARIZONA

CALIFORNIA

COLORADO

HAWAII

IDAHO

MONTANA

NEVADA

NEW MEXICO

OREGON

UTAH

WASHINGTON

WYOMING

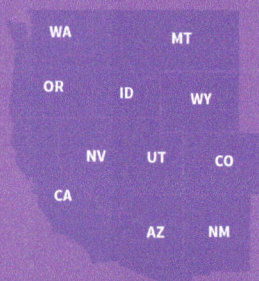

CALIFORNIA INSTITUTE OF THE ARTS (CALARTS)

Address: 24700 McBean Pkwy., Valencia, CA 91355
Website: *https://art.calarts.edu/programs/art/bfa*
Contact: *https://calarts.edu/about/contact*
Phone: (661) 255-1050
Email: admissions@calarts.edu

COST OF ATTENDANCE:

Tuition & Fees: $53,466 | **Additional Expenses:** $20,792
Total: $74,258

Financial Aid: https://calarts.edu/tuition-and-financial-aid/financial-aid/overview

ADDITIONAL INFORMATION:

Available Degree(s)

- BFA Art

Portfolio Requirement

Portfolios are required for incoming students. Submit 15-20 recent works via SlideRoom. Applicants are also strongly encouraged to submit a 30-90-second introduction video.

Scholarships Offered

CalArts offers institutional scholarships that are awarded to students based on need and merit. All awards cover tuition only. In addition, they offer endowed and annually funded scholarships.

Special Opportunities

At the start of the BFA Art program, students investigate art-historical traditions, theory, and various media. Coursework includes seminars, group critiques, and independent studies. By the third year, students pursue their independent studio projects. Most upper-level students also receive their own individual studio space.

Notable Alumni

Jeremy Blake, Nayland Blake, Ross Bleckner, Barbara Bloom, John S. Boskovich, Krista Buecking, JAmes CAsebere, Heather Cassils, Richard K. Diran, Sam Durant, Eric Fischl, Mike Kelley, Rodney McMillian, John Miller, Rubén Ortiz-Torres, Tony Oursler, Michael Polish, Gala Porras-Kim, Monique Prieto, and David Salle

LAGUNA COLLEGE OF ART AND DESIGN

Address: 2222 Laguna Canyon Rd., Laguna Beach, CA 92651
Website: *https://www.lcad.edu/drawing-painting-w-sculpture-emphasis/program/program-overview*
Contact: *https://www.lcad.edu/contact*
Phone: (949) 376-6000
Email: admissions@lcad.edu

COST OF ATTENDANCE:

Tuition & Fees: $32,600 | **Additional Expenses:** $23,979
Total: $56,579

Financial Aid: https://www.lcad.edu/admissions/tuition-financial-aid/financial-aid

ADDITIONAL INFORMATION:

Available Degree(s)

- BFA Drawing + Painting, emphasis: Sculpture

Portfolio Requirement

Portfolios are required for incoming students. Submit 12-20 recent works. LCAD suggests including observational works, life drawings, sketchbook pages that show process work, and master study works.

Scholarships Offered

The LCAD Institutional Grant is a merit-based scholarship that is based on academics and the admissions portfolio. This scholarship is renewable each year the student is at LCAD provided they remain in good academic standing. It is recommended that students apply for outside scholarships as well.

Special Opportunities

The BFA program at LCAD is grounded in classical traditions. Students are taught the necessary skills to accurately portray still life, figure, portrait, landscape, and group figures. They are also taught how to communicate visually through narrative storytelling. Furthermore, the business of art is also incorporated into the curriculum. Professional practices, marketing, and presentation are all skills that students have by the time they graduate.

Notable Alumni

Candice Bohannon, Stefan Cummings, Angela Cunningham, Matt Dickson, Alia El-Bermani, James Galindo, Frank Gonzalez, Miguel Gonzalez, Emily Gordon, Ja'Rie Gray, Michael Harnish, Adam Harrison, Jason Kowalski, Alex Krigbaum, Brianna Lee, Elizabeth McGhee, Andrew Myers, Charity Oetgen, Carolin Peters, Christopher Ramsey, Brittany Ryan, Fatima Silva, Adrienne Stein, Eric Stoner, and Jason Umfress

ALASKA

ARIZONA

CALIFORNIA

COLORADO

HAWAII

IDAHO

MONTANA

NEVADA

NEW MEXICO

OREGON

UTAH

WASHINGTON

WYOMING

WEST

ALASKA

ARIZONA

CALIFORNIA

COLORADO

HAWAII

IDAHO

MONTANA

NEVADA

NEW MEXICO

OREGON

UTAH

WASHINGTON

WYOMING

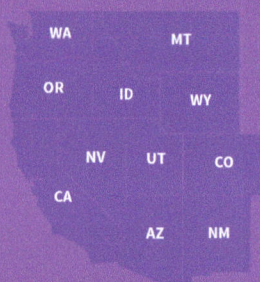

UNIVERSITY OF CALIFORNIA, LOS ANGELES

Address: 405 Hilgard Avenue, Los Angeles, CA 90095
Website: *https://www.art.ucla.edu/undergraduate-studies/*
Contact: *https://admission.ucla.edu/contact*
Phone: (310) 206-8441
Email: https://admission.ucla.edu/contact/admission-representatives

COST OF ATTENDANCE:

In-State Tuition & Fees: $13,239 | **Additional Expenses:** $22,096
Total: $35,335

Out-of-State Tuition & Fees: $42,993 | **Additional Expenses:** $22,096
Total: $65,089

Financial Aid: https://www.financialaid.ucla.edu/

ADDITIONAL INFORMATION:

Available Degree(s)

- BA Art, concentrations: Ceramics or Sculpture

Portfolio Requirement

Portfolios are required for incoming students. Submit 8-10 works.

Scholarships Offered

Students may apply for scholarships through the MyUCLA portal. Additionally, UCLA offers the Regents Scholarship for students who demonstrate academic excellence. Up to 100 are awarded per year.

Special Opportunities

Experimentation with media and critical thinking are foundational tenets of the BA program at UCLA. Students are encouraged to broaden their perceptual awareness and discuss the historical and contemporary precedents for the work they produce. UCLA houses five spacious studio classrooms that overlook Los Angeles. Six individual senior studio spaces are awarded by a portfolio review. Students also may utilize the wood shop or printmaking studio.

Notable Alumni

Amy Adler, Sara Kathryn Arledge, Glenna Avila, GAry Baseman, Edith Baumann, Slater Bradley, Vija Celmins, Coleman Collins, Jennifer Dalton, Alyce Frank, Charles Garabedian, Gilah Yelin Hirsch, Jane Jin Kaisen, Craig Kauffman, Annie Lapin, Linda Levi, Edward Meshekoff, Meleko Mokgosi, Ed Moses, Alexandra Nechita, Tameka Norriss, Raymond Pettibon, Jason Rhoades, Betye Saar, Ben Sakoguchi, Shizu Saldamando, Sarah Seager, Cindy Shih, Jan Stussy, Wu Tsang, Idelle Weber, Jan Wurm, and Richard Wyatt Jr.

UNIVERSITY OF OREGON

Address: 5249 University of Oregon, Eugene, OR 97403
Website: *https://artdesign.uoregon.edu/art/undergrad/bfa/art-concentration*
Contact: *https://admissions.uoregon.edu/contact*
Phone: (541) 346-3656
Email: admissions@uoregon.edu

COST OF ATTENDANCE:

In-State Tuition & Fees: $15,054 | **Additional Expenses:** $14,640
Total: $29,694

Out-of-State Tuition & Fees: $41,700 | **Additional Expenses:** $14,640
Total: $56,340

Financial Aid: https://financialaid.uoregon.edu/

ADDITIONAL INFORMATION:

Available Degree(s)

- BFA Art, areas: Ceramics, Jewelry & Metalsmithing, or Sculpture
- BA Art, areas: Ceramics, Jewelry & Metalsmithing, or Sculpture

Portfolio Requirement

Portfolios are not required for incoming students. However, a portfolio review is required to move onto the BFA program after completing undergraduate art coursework at the University of Oregon.

Scholarships Offered

The Architects Foundation Diversity Scholarships, need-based aid, and university-wide scholarships offer varying award amounts and opportunities. University-wide scholarships include the Stamps Scholarship (four years of full tuition, fees, room & board, and up to $12,000 in enrichment funds), the Presidential Scholarship ($36,000 over four years), Diversity Excellence Scholarship ($6500), and more.

Special Opportunities

The ceramics studio is located among a complex of art studios among the trees along the Willamette river. The ceramics program emphasizes an investigative approach to understanding material, methods, and theories. The jewelry and metalsmithing program hosts regular, visiting artists such as Beverly Penn, Bettina Speckner, Maria Phillips, and other notable artists. The sculpture program is intimate, allowing for an intensive and immersive working environment alongside peers and faculty.

Notable Alumni

Gordon GIlkey, LaVerne Krause, Suzie Liles, Susan Lowdermilk, Eric Norstad, Joe Sacco, Heidi Schwegler, Charles Stokes, Ron Wigginton, and Russel Wong

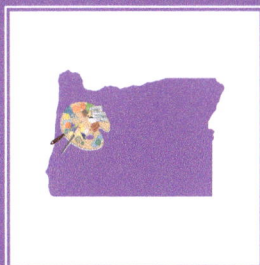

ALASKA

ARIZONA

CALIFORNIA

COLORADO

HAWAII

IDAHO

MONTANA

NEVADA

NEW MEXICO

OREGON

UTAH

WASHINGTON

WYOMING

WEST

ALASKA

ARIZONA

CALIFORNIA

COLORADO

HAWAII

IDAHO

MONTANA

NEVADA

NEW MEXICO

OREGON

UTAH

WASHINGTON

WYOMING

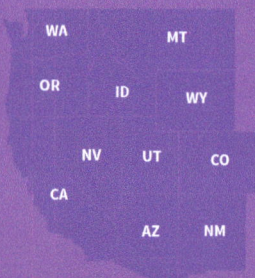

CENTRAL WASHINGTON UNIVERSITY

Address: 400 E University Way, Ellensburg, WA 98926
Website: *https://www.cwu.edu/art/bfa-studio-art*
Contact: *https://www.cwu.edu/theatre/contact-us-or-request-information*
Phone: (509) 963-1750
Email: theatre@cwu.edu

COST OF ATTENDANCE:

In-State Tuition & Fees: $7,186 | **Additional Expenses:** $18,867
Total: $26,053

Out-of-State Tuition & Fees: $23,262 | **Additional Expenses:** $18,867
Total: $42,129

Financial Aid: https://www.cwu.edu/financial-aid/

ADDITIONAL INFORMATION:

Available Degree(s)

- BFA Studio Art

Portfolio Requirement

Portfolios are required for incoming students. Submit 10 works that represent your drawing skills in different media.

Scholarships Offered

Students are encouraged to apply for scholarships via the Scholarship Central online application.

Special Opportunities

Central Washington University offers specializations in various 3D art fields, such as Ceramics, Metalsmithing, Sculpture, and Wood Design. Ceramics students may utilize the clay mixing room, a ceramics room, and various types of kilns and other equipment. Jewelry students utilize specialized equipment for jewelry-making and learn about soldering, casting, enamling, etching, electroplating, and polishing.

Notable Alumni

Jill Jones

UNIVERSITY OF WASHINGTON

Address: University of Washington, Seattle, WA 98195
Website: *https://art.washington.edu/art/undergraduate-program*
Contact: *https://admit.washington.edu/contact/*
Phone: (206) 543-9686
Email: Contact via contact link.

COST OF ATTENDANCE:

In-State Tuition & Fees: $12,076 | **Additional Expenses:** $18,564
           Total: $30,640

Out-of-State Tuition & Fees: $39,906 | **Additional Expenses:** $18,564
Total: $58,470

Financial Aid: https://www.washington.edu/financialaid/

ADDITIONAL INFORMATION:

Available Degree(s)

- BA Art, concentration: 3D4M: ceramics + glass + sculpture

Portfolio Requirement

Portfolios are not required for incoming students.

Scholarships Offered

UW offers several types of institutional aid for all students. Washington residents that show exceptional leadership and community engagement may be eligible for the Presidential Scholarship (valued at $10,000). All U.S. citizens may be eligible for the Purple & Gold Scholarship. High-need, high achieving students are eligible for the UW Diversity Scholarship ($10,000 per year for four years).

Special Opportunities

Some of the coursework Art students take include Intro to Ceramics, Intro to Sculpture, Works on Paper, Narratives in Art & Design, Color Studies, Intro to Glass, and more. An art history class is also required, and student smay choose from a variety of courses, such as: Athena to Lady Gaga: Art in the Modern Imagination, Chinese Art & Visual Culture, Art of India: Mohenjo-Daro to the Mughals, Paris Architecture, and more.

Notable Alumni

Deborah Aschheim, Bennett Bean, Nancy Carman, F. Lennox Campello, Dan Corson, Fredericka Foster, and Norie Sato

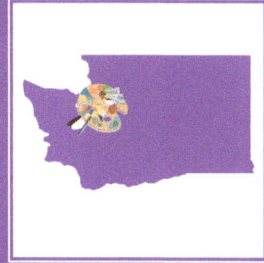

ALASKA

ARIZONA

CALIFORNIA

COLORADO

HAWAII

IDAHO

MONTANA

NEVADA

NEW MEXICO

OREGON

UTAH

WASHINGTON

WYOMING

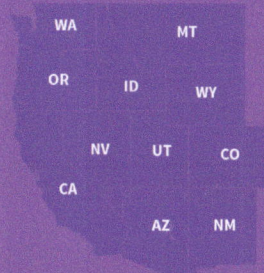

WEST

CHAPTER 16

3D ART SCHOOLS BY CITY/STATE

School	City	State
Laguna College of Art and Design	Laguna Beach	California
University of California, Los Angeles (UCLA)	Los Angeles	California
Academy of Art University	San Francisco	California
California College of the Arts	San Francisco	California
California Institute of the Arts	Valencia	California
Yale University	New Haven	Connecticut
Ringling College of Art and Design	Sarasota	Florida
University of Georgia	Athens	Georgia
Savannah College of Art and Design	Savannah	Georgia
University of Illinois Urbana-Champaign (UIUC)	Champaign	Illinois
School of the Art Institute Chicago	Chicago	Illinois
Indiana University Bloomington	Bloomington	Indiana
University of Kansas	Lawrence	Kansas
Maryland Institute College of Art	Baltimore	Maryland
Boston University	Boston	Massachusetts
Massachusetts College of Art & Design	Boston	Massachusetts
University of Massachusetts, Dartmouth	North Dartmouth	Massachusetts
University of Michigan	Ann Arbor	Michigan
College for Creative Studies	Detroit	Michigan
Rutgers, The State University of New Jersey	New Brunswick	New Jersey
Alfred University	Alfred	New York
Bard College	Annandale-On-Hudson	New York
Pratt Institute	Brooklyn	New York
SUNY New Paltz	New Paltz	New York
Columbia University	New York	New York
CUNY Hunter College	New York	New York
Fashion Institute of Technology	New York	New York
Parsons School of Design	New York	New York
School of Visual Arts	New York	New York
Rochester Institute of Technology	Rochester	New York
Syracuse University	Syracuse	New York
Cleveland Institute of Art	Cleveland	Ohio
Columbus College of Art & Design	Columbus	Ohio
Ohio State University	Columbus	Ohio
University of Oregon	Eugene	Oregon
Temple University	Philadelphia	Pennsylvania

School	City	State
University of the Arts	Philadelphia	Pennsylvania
Rhode Island School of Design	Providence	Rhode Island
University of North Texas	Denton	Texas
Virginia Commonwealth University	Richmond	Virginia
Central Washington University	Ellensburg	Washington
University of Washington	Seattle	Washington
University of Wisconsin, Madison	Madison	Wisconsin

CHAPTER 17

3D ART SCHOOLS BY AVERAGE GPA AND AVERAGE TEST SCORE

3D ART SCHOOLS BY AVERAGE GPA

School	Avg. GPA
Central Washington University	3.09
University of Massachusetts, Dartmouth	3.31
Alfred University	3.4
Temple University	3.48
Savannah College of Art and Design	3.6
SUNY New Paltz	3.6
University of Oregon	3.65
Syracuse University	3.67
Rochester Institute of Technology	3.7
Virginia Commonwealth University	3.72
Indiana University Bloomington	3.74
Boston University	3.76
Pratt Institute	3.82
University of Washington	3.82
University of Michigan	3.87
University of Wisconsin, Madison	3.87
University of California, Los Angeles (UCLA)	3.9
University of Georgia	4.02
University of Kansas	3.66
Academy of Art University	N/A *Open admissions
Bard College	N/A
California College of the Arts	N/A
California Institute of the Arts	N/A
Cleveland Institute of Art	N/A
College for Creative Studies	N/A
Columbia University	N/A
Columbus College of Art & Design	N/A
CUNY Hunter College	N/A
Fashion Institute of Technology	N/A
Laguna College of Art and Design	N/A
Maryland Institute College of Art	N/A
Massachusetts College of Art & Design	N/A
Ohio State University	N/A
Parsons School of Design	N/A
Rhode Island School of Design	N/A

School	Avg. GPA
Ringling College of Art and Design	N/A
Rutgers, The State University of New Jersey	N/A
School of the Art Institute Chicago	N/A
School of Visual Arts	N/A
University of Illinois Urbana-Champaign (UIUC)	N/A
University of North Texas	N/A
University of the Arts	N/A
Yale University	N/A

3D ART SCHOOLS BY AVERAGE SAT SCORE

School	Avg. SAT
Central Washington University	470-580 (ERW) 460-570 (M)
Alfred University	480-600 (ERW) 490-600 (M)
University of Massachusetts, Dartmouth	490-600 (ERW) 500-590 (M)
University of North Texas	530-630 (ERW) 520-610 (M)
SUNY New Paltz	530-630 (ERW) 540-630 (M)
Savannah College of Art and Design	540-640 (ERW) 500-600 (M)
Virginia Commonwealth University	540-640 (ERW) 520-610 (M)
School of Visual Arts	545-650 (ERW) 530-680 (M)
University of Oregon	550-650 (ERW) 540-640 (M)
University of Kansas	550-660 (ERW) 540-670 (M)
School of the Art Institute Chicago	560-660 (ERW) 480-600 (M)
Cleveland Institute of Art	560-680 (ERW) 510-620 (M)
Pratt Institute	570-660 (ERW) 550-680 (M)
CUNY Hunter College	580-650 (ERW) 590-690 (M)
Parsons School of Design	580-680 (ERW) 560-680 (M)
Rutgers, The State University of New Jersey	580-680 (ERW) 600-730 (M)
Indiana University Bloomington	580-700 (ERW) 560-680 (M)
Ohio State University	590-690 (ERW) 620-740 (M)
University of Washington	590-700 (ERW) 610-753 (M)
University of Illinois Urbana-Champaign (UIUC)	590-700 (ERW) 620-770 (M)
Rochester Institute of Technology	600-690 (ERW) 620-730 (M)
University of Wisconsin, Madison	610-690 (ERW) 650-770 (M)
Rhode Island School of Design	610-700 (ERW) 640-770 (M)
University of Georgia	620-700 (ERW) 600-720 (M)
Boston University	640-720 (ERW) 670-780 (M)

School	Avg. SAT
University of California, Los Angeles (UCLA)	640-740 (ERW) 640-790 (M)
University of Michigan	660-740 (ERW) 680-780 (M)
Columbia University	720-770 (ERW) 740-800 (M)
Yale University	720-780 (ERW) 740-800 (M)
Syracuse University	N/A
Columbus College of Art & Design	N/A *Test optional
Fashion Institute of Technology	N/A *Test optional
University of the Arts	N/A *Test optional
College for Creative Studies	N/A *Not required
Academy of Art University	N/A *Open admissions
Bard College	N/A *Test optional
California College of the Arts	N/A *Test optional
California Institute of the Arts	N/A *Test optional
Laguna College of Art and Design	N/A *Test optional
Maryland Institute College of Art	N/A *Test optional
Massachusetts College of Art & Design	N/A *Test optional
Ringling College of Art and Design	N/A *Test optional
Temple University	N/A *Test optional

3D ART SCHOOLS BY AVERAGE ACT SCORE

School	Avg. ACT C
Central Washington University	17-24
Cleveland Institute of Art	19-27
University of Massachusetts, Dartmouth	20-26
Savannah College of Art and Design	20-27
University of North Texas	20-27
Alfred University	21-27
Virginia Commonwealth University	21-28
University of Kansas	21-29
School of the Art Institute Chicago	22-25
University of Oregon	22-29
School of Visual Arts	23-27
SUNY New Paltz	24-29
Pratt Institute	25-30
CUNY Hunter College	25-31
Rutgers, The State University of New Jersey	25-32
Parsons School of Design	26-30

School	Avg. ACT C
Indiana University Bloomington	26-32
Ohio State University	26-32
Rhode Island School of Design	27-32
University of Georgia	27-32
University of Wisconsin, Madison	27-32
University of Illinois Urbana-Champaign (UIUC)	27-33
University of Washington	27-33
University of California, Los Angeles (UCLA)	27-34
Rochester Institute of Technology	28-33
Boston University	30-34
University of Michigan	31-34
Yale University	33-35
Columbia University	33-35
Syracuse University	N/A
Columbus College of Art & Design	N/A *Test optional
Fashion Institute of Technology	N/A *Test optional
University of the Arts	N/A *Test optional
College for Creative Studies	N/A *Not required
Academy of Art University	N/A *Open admissions
Bard College	N/A *Test optional
California College of the Arts	N/A *Test optional
California Institute of the Arts	N/A *Test optional
Laguna College of Art and Design	N/A *Test optional
Maryland Institute College of Art	N/A *Test optional
Massachusetts College of Art & Design	N/A *Test optional
Ringling College of Art and Design	N/A *Test optional
Temple University	N/A *Test optional

CHAPTER 18

TOP 15 SCHOOLS IN DRAWING AND PAINTING

S/N	School Name
1	Yale University
2	Rhode Island School of Design
3	School of the Art Institute of Chicago
4	Columbia University
5	Bard College
6	Boston University
7	Maryland Institute College of Art
8	University of California, Los Angeles
9	California Institute of the Arts
10	Hunter College (CUNY)
11	Pratt Institute
12	School of Visual Arts
13	Virginia Commonwealth University
14	Cranbrook Academy of Art
15	Temple University

CHAPTER 19

TOP GLASSBLOWING PROGRAMS

TOP 20 COLLEGES FOR GLASS BLOWING

Alabama

University of South Alabama – BFA Studio Art, Glass

California

California College of the Arts – BFA Glass

Central College – BFA Glass Blowing

Florida

Jacksonville University – BFA Object Design (Glass)

Illinois

Illinois State University, BFA Studio Arts, focus in Glass

Southern Illinois University – BFA, MFA in Glass

Indiana

Ball State University – BFA in Art, focus in Glass

Louisiana

Tulane University – BFA Studio Art, discipline in Glass

Massachusetts

Massachusetts College of Art and Design – BFA, MFA in Glass

New York

Alfred University – the only ABET Accredited Glass Engineering program in the US

Hartwick College – BA in Art, focus in Glass

Rochester Institute of Technology – BFA Studio Art, Glass option; MFA Glass

Ohio

Bowling Green State University – BA/BFA/MFA in Studio Art, focus in Glass

Ohio State University – BA/BFA/MFA Studio Art, area - Glass

Rhode Island

Rhode Island School of Design – BFA/MFA Glass

Pennsylvania

Temple University – BFA/MFA in Glass

Texas

University of Texas, Arlington – BFA in Glass

Virginia

Virginia Commonwealth University – BFA, MFA – Glass

Washington

University of Washington – BA/MFA in Art - 3D4M Ceramics + Glass + Sculpture

Wisconsin

University of Wisconsin, Madison – BFA in Art, area Glass and Neon

CHAPTER 20

TOP 20 GRADUATE SCHOOLS FOR SCULPTURE

S/N	School
1	Virginia Commonwealth University
2	UCLA
3	Yale University
4	Rhode Island School of Design
5	School of the Art Institute Chicago
6	Maryland Institute College of Art
7	University of Texas, Austin
8	Bard College
9	California Institute of the Arts
10	Columbia University
11	Cranbrook Academy of Art
12	New York University
13	Massachusetts Institute of Technology
14	CUNY - Hunter College
15	Pratt Institute
16	Carnegie Mellon University
17	Stanford University
18	Temple University
19	University of Georgia
20	Boston University

CHAPTER 21

TOP 40 JEWELRY & METAL ARTS PROGRAMS

TOP 40 PROGRAMS IN JEWELRY AND METAL ARTS

California

Academy of Art University, SF – AA, BFA, MA, MFA – Jewelry & Metal Arts

California College of the Arts – BFA Jewelry & Metal Arts

Cal State Long Beach – BFA Metal & Jewelry

Humboldt State University -BFA Jewelry & Small Metals

San Diego State University – MFA Jewelry & Metalsmithing

Colorado

Colorado State University – BFA in Art, Metalsmithing

Georgia

Savannah Col. of Art & Design – BFA Jewelry Design, BFA Metals & Jewelry

Illinois

Illinois State University – BFA Wood & Metals

Northern Illinois University – BFA Metalwork, Jewelry Design, & Digital Fabrication

Southern Illinois University – BFA, MFA in Jewelry & Metalsmithing

Indiana

Ball State University - BFA in Art, focus in Metal

Indiana University at Bloomington – BFA Studio Art, focus - Metals + Jewelry

Kansas

University of Kansas – BFA Metalsmithing/Jewelry

Kentucky

Eastern Kentucky University – BFA Jewelry and Metals

Maine

Maine College of Art – BFA Metalsmithing/Jewelry

Michigan

Cranbrook Academy of Art – MFA Metalsmithing

Grand Valley State University – BFA Jewelry and Metalsmithing

Kendall College of Art & Design – BFA Metals and Jewelry Design

Univ. of Michigan, Ann Arbor – BFA Metalsmithing & Jewelry focus

Massachusetts

Mass. College of Art & Design – BFA Jewelry & Metalsmithing

New York

Fashion Inst. of Technology – AAS Jewelry Design

Rochester Inst. of Technology – BFA Studio Arts, Jewelry Design & Metalsmithing option

SUNY Buffalo – BFA Metals/Jewelry

SUNY New Paltz – BA/BFA Studio Arts in Metal

Syracuse University – BFA Studio Arts, emphasis in Jewelry & Metalsmithing

North Carolina

East Carolina University – BFA/MFA Metal Design

Ohio

Bowling Green State University - BFA, MFA focus Jewelry/Metal

Miami University – BFA Metals & Jewelry Design

University of Akron – BFA Jewelry & Metalsmithing

Oregon

University of Oregon – BFA Jewelry & Metalsmithing

Pennsylvania

Arcadia University – BFA in Art, concentration in Metals and Jewelry

Edinboro University – BFA/MFA Jewelry and Metalsmithing

Temple University – BFA in Metals/Jewelry/CAD-CAM

Rhode Island

Rhode Island School of Design – BFA Jewelry + Metalsmithing

Texas

Texas Tech – BFA in Art, emphasis in Jewelry Design & Metalsmithing

University of North Texas – BFA Metalsmithing & Jewelry

Virginia

Radford University – BFA Jewelry and Metalworking

Virginia Commonwealth University – BFA, MFA – Metal/Jewelry

Washington

Central Washington University – BA Art + Design, Studio Area - Jewelry/Metalsmithing

Wisconsin

University of Wisconsin, Milwaukee – BFA Jewelry & Metalsmithing

JOURNEY TO ART, DANCE, MUSIC, THEATRE, FILM, AND FASHION SERIES

JOURNEY TO
Fashion Design
COLLEGE ADMISSIONS & PROFILES

RACHEL A. WINSTON, PH.D.

JOURNEY TO
Fashion Merchandising
COLLEGE ADMISSIONS & PROFILES

RACHEL A. WINSTON, PH.D.

JOURNEY TO
Costume Design & Technical Theatre
COLLEGE ADMISSIONS & PROFILES

RACHEL A. WINSTON, PH.D.

JOURNEY TO
Theatre and the Dramatic Arts
COLLEGE ADMISSIONS & PROFILES

RACHEL A. WINSTON, PH.D.

JOURNEY TO
Musical
Theatre
COLLEGE ADMISSIONS & PROFILES

STAGE DOOR

RACHEL A. WINSTON, PH.D.

JOURNEY TO
Architecture
COLLEGE ADMISSIONS & PROFILES

RACHEL A. WINSTON, PH.D.

JOURNEY TO
Photography
COLLEGE ADMISSIONS & PROFILES
FASHION, SPORTS, ART, TRAVEL, & JOURNALISM

RACHEL A. WINSTON, PH.D.

JOURNEY TO
Illustration
and
Comic Book Design
COLLEGE ADMISSIONS & PROFILES

RACHEL A. WINSTON, PH.D.

JOURNEY TO
Drawing
and
Painting
COLLEGE ADMISSIONS & PROFILES

RACHEL A. WINSTON, PH.D.

JOURNEY TO
Industrial &
Product Design
COLLEGE ADMISSIONS & PROFILES

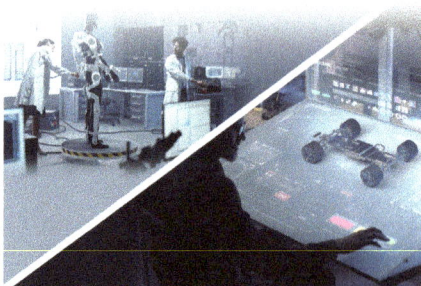

RACHEL A. WINSTON, PH.D.

JOURNEY TO
3-D
Art & Design
COLLEGE ADMISSIONS & PROFILES
SCULPTURE, CERAMICS,
GLASS, & JEWELRY DESIGN

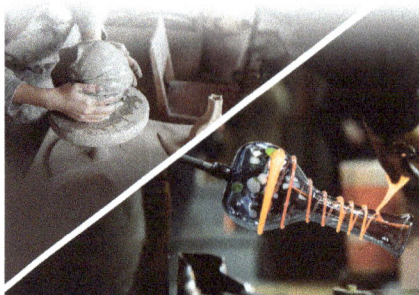

RACHEL A. WINSTON, PH.D.

JOURNEY TO
Graphic Design,
Advertising,
& Public Relations
COLLEGE ADMISSIONS & PROFILES

RACHEL A. WINSTON, PH.D.

JOURNEY TO
Film Directing & Production
COLLEGE ADMISSIONS & PROFILES
FILM, TELEVISION, & MEDIA ARTS

RACHEL A. WINSTON, PH.D.

JOURNEY TO
Screenwriting & Film and Cinema Studies
COLLEGE ADMISSIONS & PROFILES
WRITING, CULTURE, HISTORY, & CRITICAL ANALYSIS

RACHEL A. WINSTON, PH.D.

JOURNEY TO
Newspaper, Radio, & Broadcast Journalism
COLLEGE ADMISSIONS & PROFILES
TELEVISION, RADIO, PRINT & NEW MEDIA

RACHEL A. WINSTON, PH.D.

JOURNEY TO
Dance
COLLEGE ADMISSIONS & PROFILES
BALLET, CONTEMPORARY, MODERN, JAZZ,
TAP, HIP HOP, THEATRICAL, & BALLROOM

RACHEL A. WINSTON, PH.D.

220

JOURNEY TO
Psychology
COLLEGE ADMISSIONS & PROFILES
CLINICAL, COUNSELING, SPORTS, & EDUCATIONAL

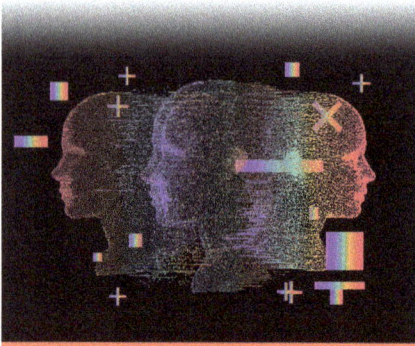

RACHEL A. WINSTON, PH.D.

JOURNEY TO
Forensic Psych.,
Crime Scene,
& Cybercrime
COLLEGE ADMISSIONS & PROFILES

RACHEL A. WINSTON, PH.D.

JOURNEY TO
Animation &
Game Design
COLLEGE ADMISSIONS & PROFILES

RACHEL A. WINSTON, PH.D.

JOURNEY TO
Law &
Criminal Justice
COLLEGE ADMISSIONS & PROFILES

RACHEL A. WINSTON, PH.D.

JOURNEY TO
Sports Management,
Athletic Training,
& Kinesiology
COLLEGE ADMISSIONS & PROFILES

RACHEL A. WINSTON, PH.D.

JOURNEY TO
Business
COLLEGE ADMISSIONS & PROFILES
ACCOUNTING, ENTREPRENEURSHIP, FINANCE, MANAGEMENT, MARKETING, & REAL ESTATE

RACHEL A. WINSTON, PH.D.

Live your dreams today remembering that discipline is the bridge between dreams and achievement!

"We believe in the American Dream that all people rich or poor can go as far in life as their talents and persistence will take them."
– Lizard Publishing Vision

At Lizard, we help you make your dreams come true.

CONTACT INFORMATION

Phone: 949-833-7706
E-mail: collegeguide@yahoo.com
Website: collegelizard.com and Lizard-publishing.com

222

COMPREHENSIVE HEALTH CARE SERIES

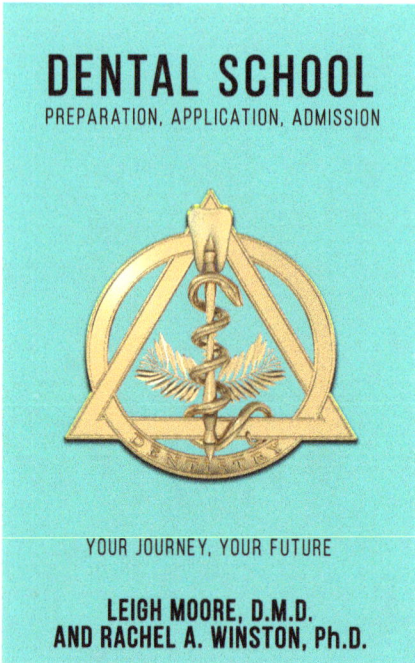

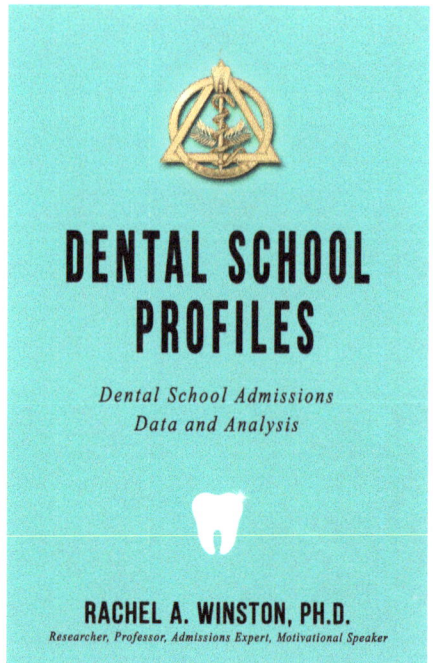

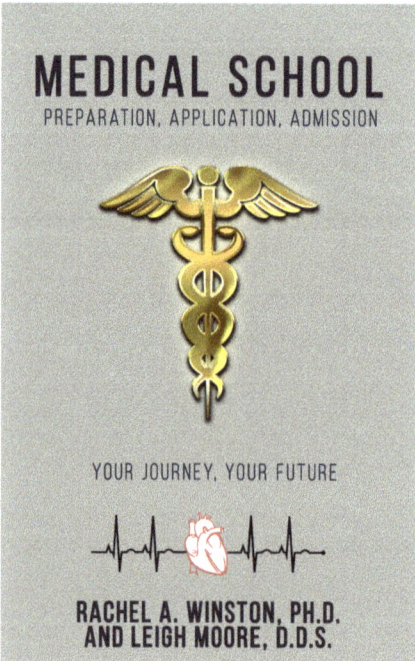

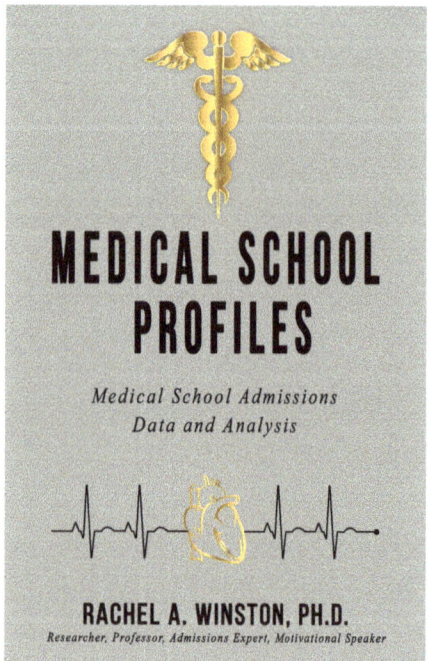

DENTAL SCHOOL
PREPARATION, APPLICATION, ADMISSION

YOUR JOURNEY, YOUR FUTURE

**LEIGH MOORE, D.M.D.
AND RACHEL A. WINSTON, Ph.D.**

DENTAL SCHOOL PROFILES

*Dental School Admissions
Data and Analysis*

RACHEL A. WINSTON, PH.D.
Researcher, Professor, Admissions Expert, Motivational Speaker

MEDICAL SCHOOL
PREPARATION, APPLICATION, ADMISSION

YOUR JOURNEY, YOUR FUTURE

**RACHEL A. WINSTON, PH.D.
AND LEIGH MOORE, D.D.S.**

MEDICAL SCHOOL PROFILES

*Medical School Admissions
Data and Analysis*

RACHEL A. WINSTON, PH.D.
Researcher, Professor, Admissions Expert, Motivational Speaker

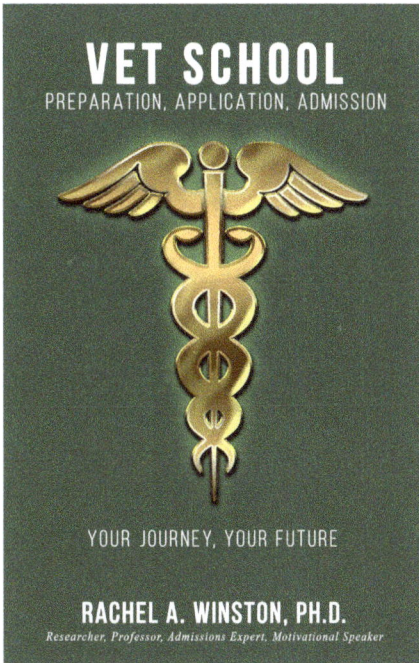

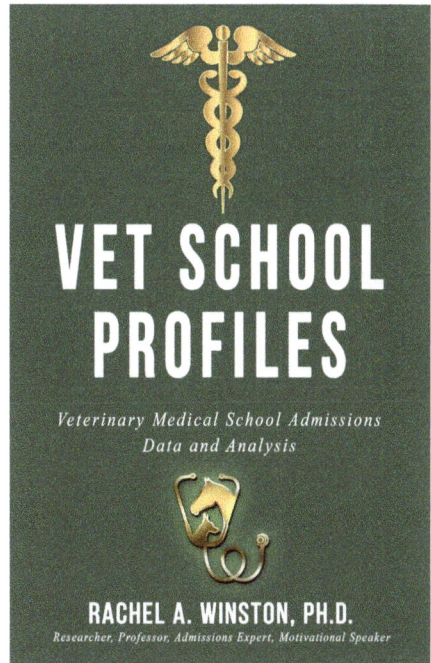

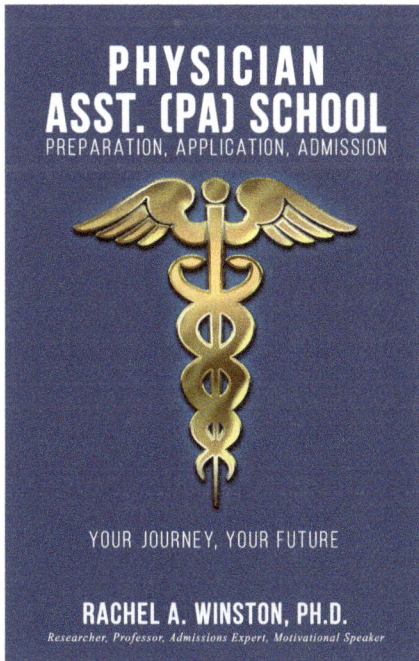

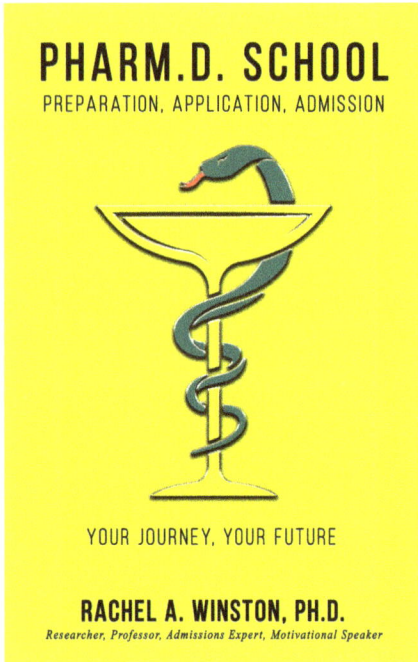

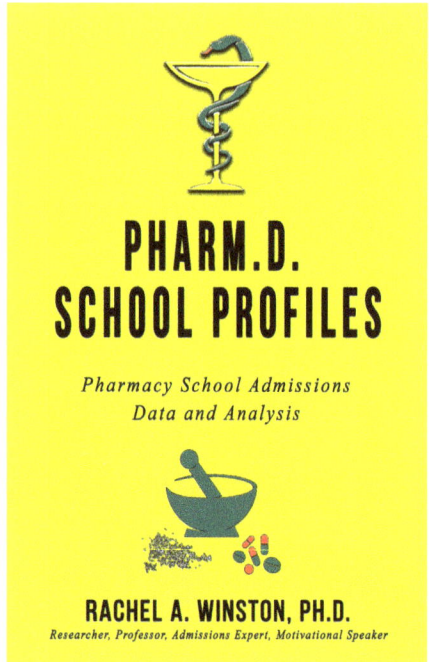

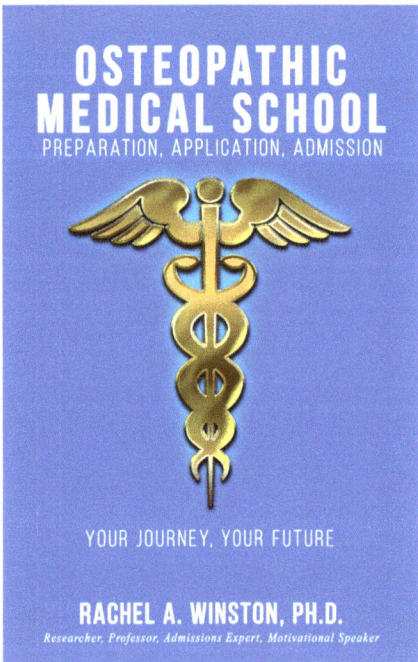

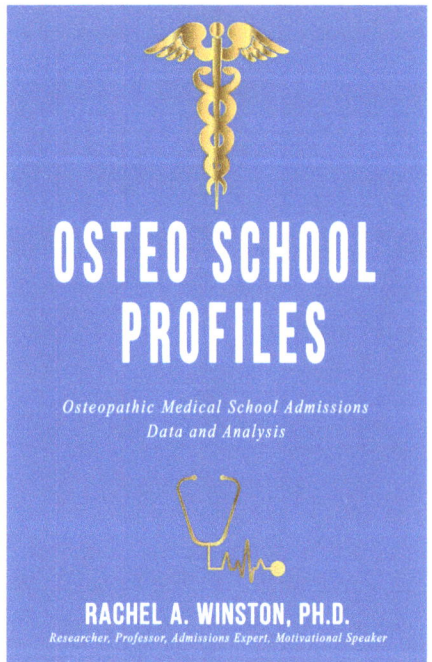

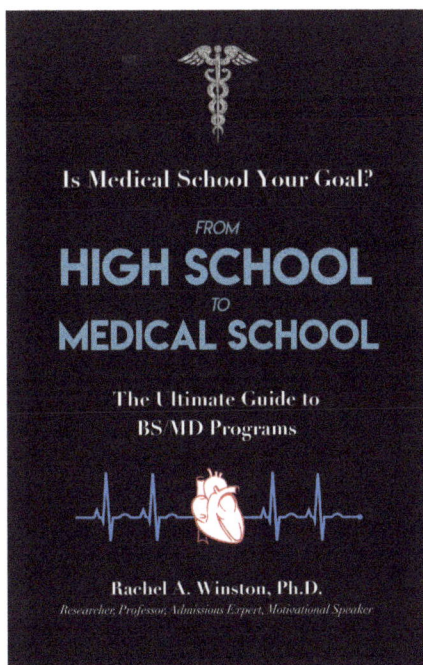

This comprehensive healthcare series is designed in full color to aid the growing number of applicants seeking clear, comprehensive materials. As a college admissions expert and former UCLA College Counseling Certificate Program faculty member, Dr. Winston is dedicated to helping students obtain the information they need.

FOR MORE INFORMATION

bsmdguide.com

medschoolexpert.com

Purchase books at Lizard-publishing.com

SERVICES OFFERED BY LIZARD EDUCATION:

- College Counseling
- Admissions News/Resources
- Essay Support and Editing
- Interview Preparation
- Road Trips to Visit Colleges
- Career Planning/Majors/ Resumes
- BS/MD, BS/DO, BS/JD, BS/DDS
- Medical School
- Graduate School (Masters & Doctorate)
- Film Studio and Editing
- Portfolio Assistance/SlideRoom
- Athletics Recruiting/Highlight Films
- International Admissions/Visa/ TOEFL
- Financial Aid and Scholarships
- UCs, Ivy Leagues, and Colleges Nationwide
- Book Publishing
- Engineering, Robotics, STEM
- Art Portfolios

Email: collegeguide@yahoo.com

Website: collegelizard.com

LIZARD

INDEX

Symbols

2D 9, 26, 105

3D i, v, vii, 2, 3, 4, 7, 9, 10, 14, 26, 39, 42, 50, 51, 52, 53, 61, 66, 92, 99, 100, 105, 120, 127, 145, 152, 160, 163, 168, 171, 179, 194, 196, 200, 201, 202, 203

4D 3, 146, 148

A

AA 43, 55, 56, 57, 59, 60, 61, 62, 63, 215

Accredited 40

ACT 66, 75, 76, 79, 81, 130, 131, 132, 133, 134, 158, 159, 160, 174, 175, 184, 185, 186, 203, 204

admissions ii, v, vi, vii, 14, 40, 49, 66, 68, 69, 71, 74, 75, 76, 77, 78, 79, 80, 81, 82, 83, 85, 100, 101, 102, 104, 136, 137, 138, 140, 141, 142, 143, 144, 145, 147, 148, 149, 150, 151, 152, 153, 154, 163, 164, 165, 166, 167, 168, 169, 171, 176, 178, 180, 184, 188, 189, 190, 191, 193, 201, 203, 204, 223

Aesthetic 8

Animation 25, 26, 28, 29, 31, 33, 34, 36, 37, 209, 210

AP 57, 61, 66, 68, 74, 76, 79, 83

Application 66, 78, 79, 93, 103, 104, 105

Aart therapy 16, 19

Auburn University 25

B

BA 44, 46, 47, 55, 56, 57, 58, 59, 60, 61, 62, 63, 68, 69, 105, 130, 131, 136, 142, 143, 158, 163, 165, 185, 186, 192, 193, 195, 216

Bachelor's Degree 45, 62, 108, 109, 110

Bard College 40, 129, 131, 142, 197, 201, 203, 204, 207, 213

BFA 32, 43, 44, 46, 47, 50, 51, 55, 56, 58, 59, 60, 61, 62, 63, 100, 103, 104, 105,

130, 131, 132, 133, 134, 137, 138, 139, 140, 141, 144, 145, 146, 147, 148, 149, 150, 151, 152, 153, 154, 158, 159, 160, 162, 163, 164, 165, 166, 167, 168, 169, 170, 171, 174, 175, 176, 177, 178, 179, 180, 181, 184, 185, 188, 189, 190, 191, 193, 194, 215, 216
Boston College 30, 48
Brown University 35

C

California State Universities 78
Carnegie Mellon University 34, 42, 213
Ceramics 14, 24, 26, 51, 52, 104, 111, 127, 137, 147, 149, 152, 162, 169, 171, 186, 193, 194, 195
Christ the Redeemer 3
Clemson University 35
CLEP 61, 66
Coalition Application 66, 78, 79
Coca Cola Scholarship 96
Columbia University 33, 40, 129, 131, 143, 197, 201, 203, 204, 207, 213
Comcast NBCUniversal 96
Common App 78, 79, 138
Common Application 66, 78, 103, 104, 105
Cornell University 33
COVID-19 101, 111
CSS Profile 81, 82, 93

D

Deferred 66, 67
DEMOGRAPHICS 101
DigiPen Academy 37, 210
Distinguished Scholars Awards 97
Drexel University 20, 34

E

Early Action 67, 76, 81, 130
Early College Program 29
Early Decision 67, 76, 77, 81, 130, 131, 158, 159, 174, 175, 184, 185

Emory University 28
Employment 108, 110, 120, 167
Essays vi, vii, 66, 74, 78, 79, 94

F

Facebook 111, 119
FAFSA 82, 92, 93, 144, 146, 154, 168
Fashion 17, 25, 29, 33, 41, 44, 109, 129, 132, 145, 197, 201, 203, 204, 216, 218
Financial Aid 67, 136, 137, 138, 139, 140, 141, 142, 143, 144, 145, 146, 147, 148, 149, 150, 151, 152, 153, 154, 162, 163, 164, 165, 166, 167, 168, 169, 170, 171, 176, 177, 178, 179, 180, 181, 188, 189, 190, 191, 192, 193, 194, 195, 223
Florida Atlantic University 28

G

Gates Millennium Scholarship 95
Georgetown University 27
George Washington University 20, 27
Georgia Institute of Technology 28
Georgia Tech 48
GE-Reagan Foundation Scholarship 96
Glass Blowing 46
Global Solutions Lab 34
Gloria Barron Prize for Young Heroes 96

H

Harvard University 31
Hispanic Scholarship Fund 95
Homo sapiens 8

I

Ice Art Championships 2
Ice Festival 2
Ice Magic 2

Illinois Institute of Technology 29
Illustration 25, 28, 33
Instagram 111, 119
Interactive Global Simulation 34
Interlochen 32
Iinternships 2, 24, 37, 51, 58, 62, 66, 71, 80, 85, 88, 92, 111, 112, 146, 148, 210
Interview 223
Iowa State University 30

J

Jewelry 13, 43, 44, 45, 50, 51, 130, 132, 133, 134, 138, 145, 147, 148, 151, 152, 154, 158, 159, 164, 165, 166, 169, 174, 175, 177, 178, 180, 184, 185, 189, 193, 194, 215, 216
Jumpstart 26

K

K-12 Educator Scholarship 97
Kansas City Art Institute 41
Kid Architecture 29

L

Laguna College of Art & Design 26, 41
Paul Landowski 3
Liberal arts vi, 51, 52, 56, 57, 68, 147
Licensed Creative Arts Therapist 19
Licensed Professional Clinical Counselor 19
LinkedIn 119, 121

M

Maryland Institute College of Art 21, 30, 40, 41, 47, 173, 174, 179, 197, 201, 203, 204, 207, 213
Massachusetts College of Art & Design 31, 129, 130, 138, 197, 201, 203, 204
Massachusetts Institute of Technology 31, 42, 213
Master's 19, 59, 60, 63, 73, 110
Maywood University 20, 34
Metal Arts 43, 45, 50, 184, 189, 215
Metalsmithing 43, 44, 45, 50, 51, 130, 133, 134, 138, 151, 154, 165, 166, 175,

180, 185, 193, 194, 215, 216

Metaverse 3, 9, 15, 21, 116

MFA 43, 44, 46, 47, 50, 51, 55, 56, 59, 60, 63, 215, 216

MICA 30, 174, 179

N

NAACP 24, 95

National Center for Educational Statistics 18, 57, 62

NCES ii, 18, 57, 58, 62

Networking 117, 119

New Jersey Institute of Technology 32

New York University 20, 33, 100, 103, 213

Northwestern University 29

O

Occupational Outlook Handbook 108, 111

Ohio State University 46, 157, 160, 170, 197, 201, 202, 204

P

Pandemic 16, 40, 53, 69, 75, 76, 84, 85, 112

Parsons School of Design 33, 41, 42, 100, 129, 197, 201, 202, 203

Pennsylvania State University 34

Pinterest 111, 119

Portfolio 26, 27, 28, 29, 33, 34, 96, 101, 103, 130, 131, 132, 133, 134, 136, 137, 138, 139, 140, 141, 142, 143, 144, 145, 146, 147, 148, 149, 150, 151, 152, 153, 154, 158, 159, 160, 162, 163, 164, 165, 166, 167, 168, 169, 170, 171, 174, 175, 176, 177, 178, 179, 180, 181, 184, 185, 186, 188, 189, 190, 191, 192, 193, 194, 195, 223

Pratt Institute 40, 41, 42, 94, 129, 132, 147, 197, 201, 202, 203, 207, 213

President's Volunteer Service Award 70

Printmaking 105, 143, 164

Purdue Univ.-IUPUI (IN) 20

Q

Questbridge Scholarship 95

R

REA 48, 76, 130

Renaissance Kids 32

Rensselaer Polytechnic University 33

Restricted Early Action 76

Rhode Island School of Design 35, 40, 41, 42, 44, 46, 95, 100, 104, 129, 134, 154, 198, 201, 202, 204, 207, 213, 216

Ringling College of Art and Design 21, 28, 173, 197, 202, 203, 204

RISD 92, 95, 102, 104, 134, 154

Rrobotics 71, 94

Rochester Institute of Technology 46, 50, 129, 133, 148, 197, 201, 202, 204

Roger Williams University 35

ROTC 97

S

San Diego State University 43, 215

SAT 66, 75, 76, 79, 81, 130, 131, 132, 133, 134, 158, 159, 160, 174, 175, 184, 185, 186, 202, 203

Savannah College of Art & Design 28, 41, 174, 177

SCAD 28, 95, 173, 174, 177

Scholarships 25, 81, 96, 97, 136, 137, 138, 139, 140, 141, 142, 143, 144, 145, 146, 147, 148, 149, 150, 151, 152, 153, 154, 162, 163, 164, 165, 166, 167, 168, 169, 170, 171, 176, 177, 178, 179, 180, 181, 188, 189, 190, 191, 192, 193, 194, 195, 223

School of Creative & Performing Arts 26, 33, 36, 209

School of the Art Institute of Chicago 29, 41, 42, 100, 104, 158, 162, 207

SCI-Arc 26

Sculpture 3, 13, 26, 33, 34, 47, 50, 51, 105, 130, 131, 132, 133, 134, 136, 137, 138, 139, 140, 141, 143, 144, 147, 148, 149, 150, 151, 152, 153, 154, 158, 159, 160, 162, 163, 164, 168, 169, 170, 174, 175, 177, 178, 179, 180, 181, 184, 185, 188, 189, 191, 192, 193, 194, 195, 212

SlideRoom 79, 104, 105, 137, 139, 141, 146, 147, 148, 149, 152, 154, 166, 167, 168, 176, 177, 189, 190, 223

Snow Festival 2

Snow Hotel 3

Snow Village 3

SOCAPA 26, 33, 36, 209
Southern Illinois University 20, 29, 43, 46, 215
Standardized test 74
Statues 3
Storytelling 9, 191
Ssummer programs 24, 33, 37, 210
Summer Studio 27
Sustainability 34
Syracuse University 34, 44, 51, 95, 129, 133, 151, 197, 201, 203, 204, 216

T

Target Scholarship 96
Temple University 19, 35, 40, 44, 46, 129, 134, 152, 197, 201, 203, 204, 207, 213, 216
Texas Tech 36, 44, 209, 216
Thurgood Marshall College Fund 95
Tufts University 31
Tuskegee University 25
Twitter 119

U

UCLA v, vi, 26, 74, 183, 185, 192, 197, 201, 203, 204, 213, 223
University of Arkansas 25
University of California, Los Angeles 40, 183, 185, 192, 197, 201, 203, 204, 207
University of Chicago vi, 30
University of Florida 28
University of Houston 36, 209
University of Illinois 29, 157, 158, 163, 197, 202, 204
University of Massachusetts Amherst 31
University of Memphis 35
University of Miami 28
University of Michigan 32, 157, 159, 167, 197, 201, 203, 204
University of Missouri 32
University of Nebraska 32
University of Notre Dame 30
University of Oklahoma 34
University of Oregon 44, 183, 185, 193, 197, 201, 202, 203, 216

University of Tennessee 35
University of Texas at Austin 36, 209
University of Washington 47, 183, 186, 195, 198, 201, 202, 204
University of Wisconsin 37, 44, 47, 157, 160, 171, 198, 201, 202, 204, 210, 216
USC Summer 26

V

Virginia Commonwealth 40, 44, 46, 47, 51, 173, 175, 181, 198, 201, 202, 203, 207, 213, 216
Virginia Tech 37, 210
Virtual reality 28

W

WAITLISTS 85
Washington University in St. Louis 32, 100, 105
Wonderworks 36, 209

X

Xian 3

Y

Yale University 40, 47, 129, 130, 136, 197, 202, 203, 204, 207, 213
Youth Design Boston 31

Z

Zoom 102

www.ingramcontent.com/pod-product-compliance
Lightning Source LLC
Chambersburg PA
CBHW052016030426
42335CB00026B/3170